A WITNESS FOR EVER

All blessings, Shirley.

In His love.

Michael Cassidy

Ps. 20:4-5 !

Also by Michael Cassidy

**Bursting the Wineskins
Chasing the Wind
The Passing Summer
The Politics of Love**

A Witness For Ever

The Dawning of Democracy in South Africa

Stories behind the Story

Michael Cassidy

Hodder & Stoughton

LONDON SYDNEY AUCKLAND

First published in Great Britain 1995

10 9 8 7 6 5 4 3 2 1

British Library Cataloguing in Publication Data
A record for this book is available from the British Library

ISBN 0 340 63032 9

Typeset by Hewer Text Composition Services, Edinburgh
Printed and bound in Great Britain by
Cox & Wyman Ltd, Reading, Berks

Hodder and Stoughton Ltd
A Division of Hodder Headline PLC
338 Euston Road
London NW1 3BH

For all in church and state and society who laboured for the new South Africa

and

For all who by prayer and faith enabled that miracle to happen

And now, go, write it before them on a tablet, and inscribe it in a book, that it may be for the time to come as a witness for ever.

Isaiah 30:8 (RSV)

Inasmuch as many have undertaken to compile a narrative of the things which have been accomplished among us . . . it seemed good to me also, having followed all things closely for some time past, to write an orderly account for you.

Luke 1:1–3 (RSV)

There are also many other signs and miracles . . . which are not written in this book. But these are written in order that you may believe . . .

John 20:30–1 (Amplified Bible)

Contents

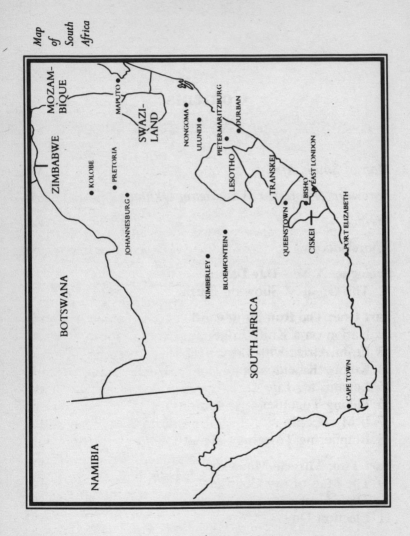

Map of South Africa

Foreword

by Professor Washington Okumu

There is a prevailing world view in the West that tends to emphasise economic and materialistic dimensions of life at the expense of the spiritual. The adherents to this world view have accommodated to their detriment an intolerance for that which is spiritual. The co-existence of secular Western thought and sacred religious fervour as influences in the corridors of power in Western capitals is often characterised by an uneasy truce, which in times of crisis degenerates into a contempt for the spiritual. This may be germane to the lapses that have become an integral part of the articulation, implementation and overall comprehension of Western foreign policy, especially in its relations with Third World Nations.

In many Third World, and particularly African societies, the spiritual dimension of life forms an integral part of the 'whole', and is incomprehensible when fragmented from it – that is, if the 'whole' in some of these societies has not yet been deliberately compartmentalised to suit the conveniences of technological advancement, industrialisation, and modernisation, which characterise many Western societies. The deeply spiritual psyches of many Third World peoples make them more amenable to accepting from and attributing extraordinary occurrences to the divine. One hopes that the Third World peoples will not only retain this quality, but will in time help the more

industrial and technologically advanced Western societies
to regain it.

It is in this context that I consider this book a path-
breaking work, particularly in its explanation to the world
of the vital spiritual and religious significance associated
with the events which culminated in my being privileged
to play a role in the achievement of the miraculous breakthrough in the South African peace process, which had
defied earlier attempts at resolution. Immediately after
the signing of the Peace (Election) Agreement in Pretoria
on 19 April 1994 by President Nelson Mandela, Deputy
President F.W. de Klerk, Minister for Home Affairs Dr
Mangosuthu Buthelezi, and myself as a witness, the
international and national media, including newspapers,
radio and television, acclaimed the event as a miracle!

The magnitude of the miracle is even more pronounced
by the involvement in the peace process of four Nobel
Peace Prize laureates, namely, Dr Henry Kissinger, Archbishop Desmond Tutu, President Nelson Mandela and
Deputy President F.W. de Klerk. Each of these statesmen
set themselves the task of brokering peace in a country
which, although considered the most powerful in Africa,
if not in the Third World, had had many centuries of
racial conflict which many thought would not end without
a major bloodbath. That the breaking out of civil war
was still imminent under these circumstances, but was
averted at the eleventh hour, can only be attributed to
the intervention of Almighty God, blessing our humble
efforts.

This book has endeavoured, in the most simple, and yet
telling and straightforward way, to narrate the spiritual
dimension of this amazing story. Michael Cassidy has
in this narration taken advantage of his unique position
as an outside witness and a participant in some of the
events, leading to the successful breakthrough in the
negotiations, to trace the 'thread' of the Holy Spirit
working through mortal men and women to accomplish

God's eternal purposes for His honour and glory. Obviously, the intricate details of the negotiations, which
resulted in the signing of the Peace (Election) agreement,
cannot be divulged now because negotiations are still
continuing to tidy up some of the remaining constitutional problems. The preconditions for any successful
peaceful negotiations depend on confidentiality and trust.
However, one day when I have the freedom to give
an account of the practical details which underpinned
all these happenings, it shall bear further testimony to
God's incredible and timely intervention in the 'weaving
of the mosaic' that brought about the peace in South
Africa.

I will not spoil the author's telling of the inexplicable
events at Lanseria Airport when all seemed lost (chapter
10). The question pre-occupying many minds is why they
happened. In my view, Dr Buthelezi was right when, in his
press statement on the occasion of the signing of the Peace
(Election) Agreement, he said, 'I told Professor Okumu
that my forced return was a God-send.'

In 1986, South Africa was on the verge of civil war
and revolution, as a result of a long period of conflict
and alienation between the races. Thousands of people had been killed, and the conflict seemed set to
get worse, and to last a long time. The cause of the
conflict was generally agreed to be the government's
policy of apartheid. It was during the same year that the
Commonwealth Group of Eminent Persons, led jointly
by Malcolm Fraser (former Prime Minister of Australia)
and General Olusegun Obasanjo (former Head of State
of Nigeria), offered everything they could, by way of
integrity, humanity, compassion, understanding and wide
political experience, to hold back the darkening storm.
Providentially, the country did not then degenerate into
civil war, but it was quite clear that the group had not
succeeded in the mission it had set out to accomplish. In
their report, however, the group acknowledged that none

of them had been prepared for the full reality of apartheid. As a contrivance of social engineering, apartheid was awesome in its cruelty. It was achieved and sustained only through force, which resulted in the creation of human misery, deprivation and the blighting of millions of innocent lives. The Reconstruction and Development Programme, which is the linchpin of President Nelson Mandela's Government of National Unity, has described apartheid's legacy in terms as stark as these.

So the question often asked is: 'How did the peoples of one of the most richly endowed countries in the world come to adopt so inefficient a social arrangement, and why did they persist with it when all the world could see it was not working?' The great miracle is that this system which had lasted for centuries (and not only since 1948 when the National Party came into power) could be ended relatively peacefully. I say relatively peacefully because, although a lot of blood had been shed during the nationalist struggle and between various political parties jostling for power, it has been estimated that more than a million people would have died if the April 1994 elections had gone ahead without the participation of the Inkatha Freedom Party. The Zulu King, Goodwill Zwelithini, told me that the difference between the Zulu war of 1879 and the one averted prior to the April 1994 elections was that modern sophisticated weapons would have been deployed in the 1994 civil war, whereas only bows and arrows were used in the 1879 war. With such proportions of human lives involved, the South African conflict would have made the 1994 Rwandan civil war look like a Sunday School picnic.

As Michael Cassidy vividly narrates in this book, the deck was really stacked against anyone being able to do anything about the South African situation, especially when Dr Henry Kissinger and Lord Carrington had decided that no breakthrough could be made between the Inkatha Freedom Party and the African National

Congress. In their letters of gratitude, both Dr Kissinger and Lord Carrington said as much. Every institutional approach had been attempted, but with disastrous consequences, leading to the escalation of violent conflict and bloodshed. The approaches had acquired diminished credibility because they tended to evoke territoriality; and the accompanying land considerations inevitably led to further conflict.

In a country which for many years was beset by anarchy in the African townships and uncontrolled violence, it was gratifying to note that the days leading towards its final liberation were characterised by the creation of ordered and stable conditions. The political leaders of South Africa had finally realised that there can be no true justice without order, that is genuine order, not the kind of repressive violence of so many years of apartheid rule. But liberation in practice is never simply about justice; it is about creating conditions in society which provide the basic framework for a harmonious and fruitful human community.

I earnestly believe that all genuine friends of South Africa, who wish that country well, will do everything in their power to help this great African nation to live in peace and godly brotherhood for ever.

And it is therefore for these reasons and because of the extraordinary story it tells that I warmly commend *A Witness For Ever* to the reading public.

Professor Washington A. J. Okumu
Nairobi, Kenya
December 1944

Preface

Nothing in South Africa is predictable, and our first democratic election was certainly no exception. Some called it a negotiated revolution. Others looked a little puzzled and wondered exactly what had happened. But that South Africa came through a multi-racial election on April 26–9 1994 without civil war or even appreciable violence, was in my view a miracle. In fact even cynics in the press hailed it as such!

To be sure, no sober observer in the weeks leading up to the elections would have held out much hope for a peaceful election in South Africa. The prognosis was awful and even our optimists were talking of civil war.

Yet before the eyes of the televised world, South Africans of every shade, shape and creed queued patiently outside polling stations ready to cast their votes and have an equal share in their own future. It was a compelling happening and very extraordinary.

It is the wonder of this momentous event, and the involvement of so many people of faith in the process leading up to it, that I feel obliged to chronicle in this book. Of course there was endless blood, sweat and tears behind the election and the run-up of the years preceding it, so I can only portray one small portion of what happened.

This story therefore is only one person's unfolding of a fascinating piece of contemporary history. I was not a major player on the stage but I did scamper on to it occasionally, rather like a 'second citizen' or 'third ghost' in one of Shakespeare's plays. For the rest I was privileged in various acts of the play to enjoy a good seat in the grandstand from which to view events.

Between the scampering and the viewing, however, I came to a considered conclusion – namely that God Himself had been involved with a Dunkirk-type miracle in the way the new South Africa had been birthed.

So while it would be an impossible task to begin even to scratch beneath the surface and reveal all the pain, trauma and heartache that has been a part of this beautiful land for so long, with thousands not alive today to see the results of their struggles, nevertheless, what we need to know and remember is that it was within this mess and tragedy that God intervened and brought about something miraculous.

Of course, if one looks at South Africa from a purely secularist or materialist world view, one will simply say those clever South Africans pulled it off! But if one looks at the situation from a biblical world view, which is what I have sought here to do, then, I believe, one has to say God was involved, and that He heard the cries of His people.

That conviction gradually birthed another – fuelled by a quickening to my heart of an Old Testament Scripture to 'write it in a book that it may be for the time to come as a witness for ever' (Isa. 30:8).

You see, the developing concern in my soul was two-fold. First, that as the election of April 1994 receded into the past, the sense of the miraculous and of God's intervention which pervaded one and all at the time, including the secular press, would be replaced by a proud, possibly even rebellious spirit of self-congratulation – that we had done it all ourselves, thanks to our great ingenuity, flexibility and political skills, so that God and His mighty and merciful work would be altogether forgotten.

It is so easy to rationalise events and forget what actually happened. It is because of the possibility of this kind of spiritual amnesia that I am wanting to share about this

South African miracle so that both South Africans and others do indeed give proper thanks and credit where it is due, namely to the Living God, and do not forget that the new South Africa was born through an act of God.

My second concern was that this very spirit of proud self-congratulation, which I already discern rising in the breast of the nation, would lead us to the view that we can in fact press on into the future on our own, in our own strength, and with God politely sidelined, though possibly to be called on again like a sort of cosmic bell-boy if we hit some major new crisis. But He is not really to remain central to our national life and we would therefore turn our backs on the truth that 'Blessed is the nation whose God is the Lord' (Ps. 33:12) and ignore the other inner key to national blessing, namely that 'Righteousness exalts a nation' (Prov. 14:34). None of this is to deny or undermine the backdrop of intense hard work against which all this happened. But if we do recognise the hand of God irrevocably, we will always honour and thank Him for what He has done and keep Him central to our future national life. So, as the new South Africa was born through a gracious act of God, it needs nurturing from the same Source.

Of course, I cannot profess, nor have I aimed, to try and be a historian of the whole process by which democracy dawned in South Africa. That is beyond both my abilities and purpose. Thus, though I have sought to glean and research where I could, I cannot in the nature of things write the Mandela story, or de Klerk story, or Tutu story, or Chikane story, or Coleman story, or Buthelezi story, or McCauley story, or SACC story, or Rosenberg story, or Kriegler story, or closer to the ground, the Mrs Ndlovu story, or even the full Okumu story. I can only tell about where my little story intersected with theirs. I was a flea on a very big elephant. I can only tell my own 'flea's-eye' view of the creature.

I would like to add that throughout the telling of this tale

I have sought to maintain absolute accuracy and clarity in relaying details where they concern the involvement of other people, and of course with their permission where that seemed necessary. However, although I have sought to have every detail checked as thoroughly as possible, I realise the capacity for mistakes, and if there are any such inaccuracies then I hope any affected will accept my sincere apologies.

Finally, I do want to express very special thanks to a number of people. First, I owe a very great debt of gratitude to my assistants, Jamie Morrison and Lucy Carr, who gave themselves unstintingly over several months in the process of research, editing and advising on the text. Without Jamie and Lucy this book would not have seen the light of day.

My secretary, Colleen Smith, was a star in the firmament as usual with massive typing and word processing labours. I owe so much to her in this, as in so many other endeavours.

Yvonne Breckenridge did some very crucial interviewing of several political leaders for me. Val Pauquet was likewise generous to assist me with interviews of National Peace Accord leaders. In this regard I must thank more than forty political leaders, including President Mandela, Minister Buthelezi and Deputy President de Klerk, who read sections of the story referring to them, offered their comments, and sent good wishes for the book's success.

The manuscript was read and most helpfully critiqued in whole or in part by Calvin Cook, Nellis du Preez, Peter Kerton-Johnson, Washington and Rizpah Okumu, Danie Schutte, Derryn Hurry, Anthony Cordle, Betty Govinden, Olave Snelling and Musa Opiyo. Caesar Molebatsi also shared valuable observations and insights.

I must also extend my appreciation to Murray and Cynthia Armstrong, who allowed Jamie, Lucy and me to spend a working week at their Balgowan farm so that, in peace and quiet, we could labour undisturbed day and night. That was special.

I am thoroughly indebted to James Catford, Bryony Bénier, Annabel Robson and Tim Moyler at Hodder & Stoughton in London, all of whom have helped steer the book through to final publication. Edward England, my author's agent, and Alasdair Verschoyle at Struik Books have likewise been so helpful.

Above all, I praise God for my beloved wife, Carol, who bears with so much and makes so many sacrifices when I get caught up in a writing project.

And so I commend this story to the reading public with the hope and prayer that it will encourage and inspire and, beyond that, stand as *a witness for ever* to what God has done in South Africa in these times.

Michael Cassidy
Pietermaritzburg, October 1994

Abbreviations

AE	=	African Enterprise
ANC	=	African National Congress
APLA	=	Azanian People's Liberation Army
AVU	=	Afrikaner Volksunie
AWB	=	Afrikaner Weerstandsbeweging (Afrikaner Resistance Movement)
AZAPO	=	Azanian People's Organisation
AZAYO	=	Azanian Youth Organisation
CBM	=	Consultative Business Movement
CODESA	=	Congress for a Democratic South Africa
COSATU	=	Congress of South African Trade Unions
CP	=	Conservative Party
CREID	=	Christian Research, Education and Information for Democracy
DP	=	Democratic Party
DRC	=	Dutch Reformed Church
FA	=	Freedom Alliance
GNU	=	Government of National Unity
IDASA	=	Institute for a Democratic Alternative for South Africa
IEC	=	Independent Electoral Commission
IFP	=	Inkatha Freedom Party
KJV	=	King James Version of the Bible
KNEON	=	KwaZulu-Natal Election Observer Network
KZP	=	KwaZulu Police
NGK	=	Nederduitse Gereformeerde Kerk
NIR	=	National Initiative for Reconciliation
NP	=	National Party
NPA	=	National Peace Accord
NPI	=	Newick Park Initiative
OAU	=	Organisation of African Unity
PAC	=	Pan Africanist Congress
PACSA	=	Pietermaritzburg Agency for Christian Social Awareness
PFP	=	Progressive Federal Party
PWV	=	Pretoria-Witwatersrand-Vereeniging
RCC	=	Rustenburg Churches Conference
SACC	=	South African Council of Churches
SACOB	=	South African Chamber of Business
SACP	=	South African Communist Party
SADF	=	South African Defence Force
TEC	=	Transitional Executive Council
TPA	=	Transvaal Provincial Administration
UNISA	=	University of South Africa
WCC	=	World Council of Churches

Prologue

A NEW DAY DAWNS

1 The Greatest Show on Earth

The alarm rang. It was 3 a.m. on 10 May 1994 at the Howard Johnson hotel in Denver, Colorado. Time to wake up. Time for history. Time to turn on the TV. Time for what the local papers dubbed 'The Greatest Show on Earth'. Time to watch Nelson Mandela being inaugurated as the first black President of the Republic of South Africa.

I blinked sleep out of my eyes, switched on the lights, reached for the remote control and pushed 'power'. Yes, this moment was about power: God's and man's. The picture heaved into view with the omnipresent and seemingly ever wakeful newsman at CNN busy telling us it was all going to start happening 'any time'. When he'd said that ten times in the next hour I concluded the inauguration of Nelson Mandela, like black majority rule in South Africa generally, was arriving a little late. So what was new? After all, as Africans say, 'You whites have the watches. We have the time.' Yes, patience is an African virtue – where would we be without it? – and Western punctuality has probably been appropriately declared a false god.

WAITING

So while CNN and the world waited, I did too. Other news items flashed across the screen: tracer fire, etched in deadly pellets of light, arching across the night sky in Sarajevo; then trails of pitiful Rwandan refugees, tens of thousands of them, stumbling helplessly along a path to who knows where. And the Kagera River swirling and twirling its catastrophic cargo of bloated bodies towards Lake Victoria.

It made one's blood run cold and chilled the soul. Some said between 300,000 and 500,000 had died, surely one of the most horrendous tragedies of the century and one of its greatest crimes.

And what of my African Enterprise colleagues in Rwanda? Was my Malachie, mighty in the love of God, one of the casualties? Or precious Phoebe? Or Gaudence or Enoch? Or Jocelyn or Jemina? Poor Israel, leader of our team, and all his family were gone, brutally murdered by fellow Hutu for reaching out in reconciliation to Tutsi people. In my heart I saluted him.

Memories of being in Rwanda just weeks previously flooded back – preaching with Israel in Kigali's stadium; meeting leaders of the non-government organisations and talking about the part they could play in reconciliation; visiting refugee and displacee camps where 300,000 people, even before the latest convulsion, were mute testimony to the terrible tragedy of ethnic warfare. Yes, and then, in a country without a government but trying to form one, there was that breakfast meeting with leaders from the fourteen political parties at the home of American Ambassador David Rawson. They had all wanted to hear about South Africa and how we were going. I said we were a nation on a knife-edge. But I spoke in hope and told them about Kolobe Lodge and politicians coming to understand one another and the negotiating process. And Mandela and de Klerk. I said I believed Jesus was the answer and that the key lay in the Church. In Rwanda the Church seemed to be a sleeping giant. But it wasn't asleep in South Africa. Therein lay our hope.

Prime Minister designate Faustin Twagiramungu stood up after me and appealed to one and all to find inspiration and hope in the South African experience. He ended, 'Please convey our greetings and congratulations to Dr Mandela and Mr de Klerk. You are much blessed with those men.' Yes, we are indeed. And the greetings were conveyed.

Now in Denver in the small hours of the morning, I wondered. Was Faustin Twagiramungu dead or alive? And what of the others? They had all seemed so close to an answer. Like South Africa. And then tragedy and the Devil had struck and they had thrown it all away. A nation had unravelled, probably irreparably.

But, dear Lord, how close we had come to it in South Africa! We had teetered, seemingly for weeks, at the very brink of a Rwandan abyss. That we had not gone over the edge was everywhere hailed as a miracle – the South African Miracle. Even the secular press had been full of the word, though not knowing how truly they spoke, for they did not know all the stories behind the story. I wondered whether I should try to tell some of the bits I knew.

ON CAMERA

'And now we cross directly to Pretoria, South Africa,' said my CNN anchorman, 'for the inauguration of South Africa's first black president, Nelson Roli . . .' – stumble, stumble – 'Roli-lala Mandela.' Not quite, but close enough! And we were on camera before a watching world.

There were the Union Buildings, where my grandfather had once worked, set against an azure blue skyline in brilliant South African sunlight. Multiplied thousands thronged the lawns below. Not blacks or whites this time, in deadly or monotonous monochrome, but in what Desmond Tutu called 'the full colours of the rainbow'.

Military helicopters, previously symbols to blacks of white oppression, drifted across the sky pulling the new South African flag, a rainbow in itself if ever there was one.

Now the dais, jam-packed with dignitaries, in fact more than forty heads of state, and in the centre of it all Nelson Mandela, backed by a phalanx of white, probably

Afrikaner, generals – 'I've lived a long time,' I chuckled to myself – and flanked by Deputy Presidents-elect Thabo Mbeki and F.W. de Klerk. That little enigmatic smile which never leaves de Klerk's face was slightly wider, though perhaps more enigmatic than usual.

What must he be thinking, one wondered, the jailer and the prisoner, not quite changing places, but certainly in new and unfamiliar places. One sensed the euphoria, the sheer elixir of joy and uncluttered emotion in the air. It was liberation. For blacks, liberation from oppression. For whites, liberation from guilt.

And of course Professor Washington Okumu, Roving Ambassador, Extraordinary and Plenipotentiary, from Kenya, and his wife were there. And I knew that without his tireless labours, the miracle of this day would not be unfolding in peace and unbridled celebration. Oh yes, I knew that.

BAD OLD DAYS

Thabo Mbeki looked happy too. Deputy President. Could he ever have dreamed it would really happen? I remembered back to an afternoon in his home in Lusaka, Zambia, in the bad old days of P.W. Botha. Everything at that time for Thabo Mbeki spelled exile – frustration, homelessness, banishment, the struggle and trauma plus the alternating current of hope and hopelessness. I remember the nonstop puffs on his pipe and being impressed with the spirit of sweet reasonableness which seemed to rest upon the man. We ended with prayer. But not the wildest prayer of faith at that time embraced what was now before my eyes this still-dark Denver morning. I do recollect saying to my colleague David Richardson that afternoon, 'How can we waste, throw away and ban such staggering resources of human talent and giftedness?' He shook his head and blinked. Certainly no answer to that one.

Other visits to ANC exiles in Lusaka a decade ago flooded back into memory – afternoon and evening talks in a hotel room with Pallo Jordan (now Minister of Posts, Telecommunications and Broadcasting), Ruth Mompati, Alfred Nzo (now Foreign Affairs Minister), James Peters and Steve Tshwete (now Minister of Sport). One comment from Pallo Jordan I'll never forget: 'Let me tell you how I was radically politicised in 1955 in Cape Town. I was just a young fellow and government authorities came in the small hours of a most bitter winter morning and began knocking down our homes and pulling us all out for transfer to a new township called Guguletu. The winter cold was unbearable. Not only that, but we lost our freehold land rights in this move.

'In the following days as we were moved, I saw numbers of babies die of pneumonia. That was when I knew I must now oppose apartheid with all my strength and by all means at my disposal.'

It was powerful stuff and helpful indeed to my own political education, for whites could never really feel black pain unless they touched the hem of its garment through a fearless and articulate black like Pallo Jordan. I wondered now whether Ruth, Pallo, Alfred or Steve were believing their eyes at what they were caught up in on this triumphant day. The impossible dream, their wildest and most far-flung hopes were coming true. What a day! A magical, unimaginable and never-to-be-repeated moment.

CEREMONY

A tribal dancer now leaped forward towards the podium and began an animated dance and chant. The about-to-be-inaugurated President beamed. Chief Minister Mangosuthu Buthelezi smiled widely. De Klerk, now the ex-President, looked mildly mystified.

Then there were prayers: Moslem and Hindu and

Jewish. The religious playing field was level this new day. Good thing, perhaps! Our previous Constantinianism had not been healthy for the Christian Gospel. Then Desmond Tutu – moved and ecstatic and eloquent – with a powerful prayer to the God and Father of our Lord Jesus Christ.

Finally the swearing-in. Chief Justice Michael Corbett led Thabo Mbeki and F.W. de Klerk through their lines in the oath of allegiance. Each oath ended with 'So help me God'. De Klerk for his part pointedly adjusted the line there and responded in Afrikaans: 'So help my die drie-eenigde God, Vader, Seun en Heilige Gees.' (So help me the Triune God, Father, Son and Holy Spirit.) It was a powerful and unmistakable Christian testimony and I was thankful.

When Mandela said, 'So help me God', a roar rose from the crowd, a victorious cheer after years of oppressive conflict.

Said the new President in his inaugural address: 'The moment to bridge the chasms that divide us has come. The time to build is upon us. We have at last achieved our political emancipation . . . We must therefore act together as a united people, for national reconciliation, for nation-building, for the birth of a new world . . . Let there be justice for all. Let there be peace for all. Let there be work, bread, water and salt for all . . .'

He paid a touching tribute to all South Africans who had played a role in bringing about a democratic order, 'not least among them . . . my second Deputy President, the Honourable F.W. de Klerk'.

This was followed by resolution: 'Never, never and never again shall it be that this beautiful land will again experience the oppression of one by another and suffer the indignity of being the skunk of the world.'

Instead, 'We shall build a society in which all South Africans, both black and white, will be able to walk tall, without any fear in their hearts, assured of their inalienable right to human dignity – a rainbow nation at peace with itself and the world.

'Let freedom reign. The sun shall never set on so glorious an achievement. God bless Africa.'[1]

Air Force jets screamed overhead in a salute of honour and filled the sky with all the colours of the rainbow. The crowd went wild. Many blacks in the crowd, I learned later, had felt a special thrill at that moment and said to themselves and each other, 'Those jets are now ours! And they are saluting President Mandela.'

Yes, the miracle had happened. South Africa had stepped back from the edge of civil war and cataclysmic convulsion and had entered the New Day in peace and ecstasy.

But it had been a close call.

QUESTION

I snapped off the TV at 6 a.m. and lay back reflective.

Quite a party, I thought. Definitely the greatest show on earth. No argument about that. It would have been nice to be there. Not that I'd been invited, but just to be in the country. But a precious daughter's university graduation clearly had to come first, even over such a mighty moment. I had no regrets. Besides that, a ministry tour in the United States with such a world-gripping happening back home also gave opportunities for rich testimony to our God who does all things well, and even above what we can ask or think.

'But tell me,' said a radio interviewer later that day, 'what happened? All we saw was Kissinger and Carrington returning home all dejected and cast down and pronouncing cataclysm, doomsday and apocalypse for South Africa. You were the lost cause nation. Civil war looked likely to erupt. The next minute it was all on again and the elections were happening peacefully and the world was goggle-eyed. I mean, what happened? It seems miraculous.'

'It was a miracle,' I said. 'I believe God intervened. Like at Dunkirk.' And I told him some snippets of the story.

'Wow,' he replied, 'I guess so!'

Part One

THE RUN-UP TO IT ALL

2 Nation on a Knife-Edge

It was the spring of hope, it was the winter of despair.

Charles Dickens

To be sure many, many people felt the reality of a battle for the soul of South Africa and would identify with the description of the period from February 1990 to April 1994 as 'the spring of hope and the winter of despair'. Forces of light – the processes of transformation and reconciliation – and forces of darkness – intransigence, bitterness, hatred and escalating violence – seemed to be in daily collision, tearing the national psyche asunder. To pick up one's newspaper each morning was to behold a race between political conversion and national catastrophe. We were indeed a nation on a knife-edge.

It was well summarised in a chuckling utterance by former South African newspaper editor Stephen Mulholland: 'The interesting thing about South Africa is that the answer to every question is "yes". Could there be a military coup? Yes. Could there be a bloodbath? Yes. Could there be a right-wing takeover? Yes. Could there be a black Marxist takeover? Yes. Could there be peaceful evolution? Yes. Could there be more of the same with repression and reform? Yes. What about a federal system? Yes. What about Rhodesia-style hothouse economic growth? Yes. Could there be economic collapse? Yes. Do you want to stay here? Yes. Do you want to emigrate? Yes!'

Edge of the Abyss

When speaking publicly in 1991 and 1992, especially over-seas, I often likened the South African body politic pre-1990 to a vehicle which had been heading straight towards an abyss of epic Greek tragedy. But in February 1990, the vehicle on screaming wheels had taken a radical turn at the very edge of the precipice and was now trundling along parallel and precariously close to the edge. But at least we were not going straight over.

There were huge forces seeking to push us over into the canyon of catastrophe, but then there was also a positive set of forces striving to pull the vehicle away from the edge. But which set of forces would win was anybody's guess from 1990 all the way through until eight days before the election in April 1994! Again and again through those years we were illustrating Alan Paton's famous dictum: 'South Africa is a place where you hope on Monday and despair on Tuesday.' The big challenge was to get back to hoping on Wednesday.

That's pretty much how the new South Africa looked through 1992 and 1993, especially to whites: elusive, precarious and probably destined to be a mix of racial hatred, tribal convulsion and even civil war. Certainly not a place you'd want to live in.

But let's explore further. What was the good news and what was the bad? What did the light look like and what the darkness?

GOOD NEWS

One of the bits of good news through those years was that we began to see more clearly who was who in the South African political zoo. A sort of regrouping began to take place in which three clusters emerged which we might call the *reversalists*, the *reformists* and the *revolutionaries*.

The *reversalists* were those wanting to go back to

the worn and discredited ways of classical apartheid. In this grouping were the white right-wing Conservative Party (CP), led by Dr Andries Treurnicht, and the ultra-rightist Afrikaner Weerstandsbeweging, or Afrikaner Resistance Movement (AWB), led by the fiery and furious but charismatic Eugene Terreblanche. In this general cluster also would have been found some of the élites of the quasi-independent homelands of Bophuthatswana and Ciskei who had benefited from the apartheid gravy train.

Some would have wanted, though not fairly, to put certain sections at least of the Inkatha Freedom Party in this grouping, although the fit was not a neat one. The IFP was often difficult to read. It was torn by calls on the one hand to a broader South African pan-nationalism and on the other to a Zulu ethno-nationalism. Many spectating all of this wondered where the IFP would finally land up. For myself I could see no solution for South Africa unless there was some accommodation of conservative white interests and of the Zulus north of the Tugela River. That would seem to have called for a final constitution more federal than unitary in nature.

The second grouping in the country was the *reformists*. This cluster included the African National Congress (ANC) alliance – made up of the ANC, the Congress of South African Trade Unions (COSATU) and the South African Communist Party (SACP), the National Party (NP); the Democratic Party, and smaller Coloured and Indian parties.

The reformists were bound by a compelling uniformity of interests, all of them feeling they had most to gain from a satisfactory settlement. And so, locked together by fear of the awful consequences of political failure, they found themselves staggering along in awkward tandem into an uncertain and precarious future, but sure only of one thing: that the past had become distant, dangerous and undesirable. The only way forward was forward.

Third, there were the *revolutionaries* who cried out for

their 'one settler, one bullet' or for their 'million guns' to
fight their way through to a pan-Africanist superstate or
to an Afrikaner volkstaat respectively.

Political Miracle

In the down troughs of the South African roller coaster
in these years, one did indeed have to pause every now
and then to look beyond the traumas and see the political
miracle which was nevertheless in the making. After all, a
scant three or four years previously the apartheid structure
had been in place. All opponents of 'the system' were being
locked up, banned or imprisoned. The ANC and other liberation movements were in exile and their leaders labelled
terrorists or worse. A state of war effectively existed
between the government and the liberation movements.

Overseas sanctions and boycotts were in full force.
Hundreds of people were leaving every month to go into
self-imposed exile in other parts of the world. People like
my nephew, Charlie Bester, were in prison with six-year
sentences over them for defying their call-up into an
all-white South African apartheid army.

But now a scant few years later Mandela, the prisoner
and terrorist in the former government's eyes, and de
Klerk, the apartheid ideologue and former head of the
National Party in the Transvaal, were being inspected from
afar as possible joint winners of the Nobel Peace Prize.
The old pillars of apartheid were down. The ANC was
about to become effectively the government.

Twenty-six parties, from the Communists to the Conservatives, were starting to get together round a negotiating
table to chart the future. The so-called terrorists from the
past were on our television screens every night in debate or
interchange. Sanctions were in the process of being lifted.
The SABC and SATV, while formally controlled totally by
whites, and often right-wing whites at that, were now in the
process of being internally revolutionised.

Many formerly white schools were starting to be inte-
grated. Our national sports teams were starting to take to
the fields of the world after twenty-seven years of isolation
and giving even the world champion Australians a run for
their money in both cricket and rugby!

The all-white apartheid army and its conscription processes which had put my nephew into prison were likewise
being revolutionised, as moves were under way to inte-
grate into the SADF the two or three armies which had
fought in the liberation struggle.

Beyond that, our country was being invaded weekly by
musicians, dramatists, artists and sports teams from around
the world.

Strikes which had previously been illegal were now a
regular part of political life, even though often damaging
to economic progress and recovery. Freedom of assembly,
movement and political activity was the name of the game
and political marches which had previously been met with
Caspir armoured vehicles and police dogs were now so
commonplace as to risk becoming boring. Said one wag:
'The ANC have come up with a new calendar which reads:
"January, February, March, March, March!"'

All of this was beginning to add up to a political miracle
in the making. As remarkable an aspect as any was the
gradual birthing and emergence in embryonic form of a
culture of negotiation. It led prominent journalist Allister
Sparks to write in 1993:

It is time to lift our gaze from the political wrangling
and the violence that have dominated our day-to-day
news coverage and consider what has been achieved.
It is in fact amazing. Absolutely bloody amazing. In
the course of three years, 26 parties as widely divergent
and antagonistic as any on earth, have managed to
reach agreement on a range of issues that span the
whole socio-political spectrum. It is difficult enough to
imagine 26 parties reaching agreement on anything. Yet

these did it without any foreign broker or facilitator. They did not have to be brought together on the White House lawn like Yasser Arafat and Yitzhak Rabin: there has been no Chester Crocker or UNTAG Force or Vance-Owen plan. They have done it on their own without intermediaries. What is more, they have reached agreement not only on broad principles but on legalistic detail . . . I know of no historical precedent for this.[1]

Greater Realism

At the same time greater realism had set in on all sides, and this was important, following the unrealistic euphoria after Mandela's release and the unbanning of the liberation movements. People had come to see that there was no quick fix. Many were recognising that apartheid had left a horrendous legacy which could not just be shaken off overnight. Whites had sown a wind, and some dimensions at least of the whirlwind could not be avoided. Nor could we get the emotional legacy of racial alienation out of our systems just by some new bits of legislation. The starry-eyed myth which had seen South Africa as peopled by five million white demons and thirty-five million black angels had also exploded. The capacity of black people for violence, political ineptitude, rampant factionalism and for some awful acts of short-sightedness were now obvious to all. Utopian and millennial expectations had now gone. A healthy realism was in place and this was a point of political gain all round.

Whites See the Future

There was something else very interesting through these years and that is that whites were starting to see the future and come to terms with it. This was particularly evident in the horrendous tragedy of April 1993 when Chris Hani, charismatic leader of the South African Communist Party, was assassinated by a Polish immigrant, whose accomplice was a white former Member of Parliament. As over thirty million blacks rose to condemn the deed and mourn the departed, so, I believe, did multiplied whites for the first time see the handwriting clearly on the wall. They saw the power and presence of overwhelming black numbers. They saw the black military emerging into the open, effectively from underground, with all the black generals, bedecked with medals and decorations, parading in front of their people. Whites saw for the first time the VIP world of the black community. They saw an occasion well organised and carried off with astonishing dignity. They glimpsed the massive resolution in the black soul to take over the country and put to death the iniquitous system of apartheid which had so dehumanised them.

And with no white leaders anywhere in sight on television, but only Mandela addressing the nation as the heir apparent to the presidency, they saw power moving imperceptibly from the *de jure* government of President de Klerk to the *de facto* government of the ANC. In seeking to calm people, Mandela, in statesmanlike fashion, reminded blacks that it was a white Afrikaner lady and neighbour of Chris Hani who had reported the registration number of the vehicle in which the killer had escaped. He noted that it was a twenty-year-old white Afrikaner policeman, only two years in the force, who some minutes later had arrested the assassin.

As white South Africans stared into this awesome happening they saw with eyes of fire that an assassination such as this was really the work of weakness. Whites now saw, and many for the first time, where real strength and moral authority lay.

Following up on all this the white world, and probably the black as well, was stunned when a white South African court sentenced to death a white Polish immigrant and a white former Member of Parliament for the murder of a senior black communist.

Said Ken Owen of the Johannesburg *Sunday Times* on 3 October 1993: 'The new South Africa is not to come; it is already here.'

THE BAD NEWS

Even as all of this was very remarkable, however, and there was so much that was good and positive going on in the country, nevertheless there was a dark, dangerous and desperate downside.

Throughout those years from 1990 to early 1994, it seemed to me important that we should remain optimistic and hopeful. But, on the other hand, realism required one also to grasp the awesome and fearful dimensions of what we were up against.

As we tumbled into troughs, and hit hole after hole, fear, anguish, uncertainty, despair and alarm often gripped our souls. Midst all the flurry of progressive and exciting political activity, we also wondered again and again whether we were going anywhere. In many ways we seemed to be doing well politically, but also again and again we seemed completely lost as bad news threatened not only to overwhelm us, but to destroy everything positive which was happening in the country.

Fear

From 1991 and into early 1994, South Africa was a society gripped by profound fear of almost every sort.

First there was *political fear*. In a way for whites this was nothing new because the apartheid edifice had been born out of fear of being overwhelmed by blacks. In the 1940s Dr D.F. Malan had played on this with his warning cry of 'swart Gevaar' (the black danger) and on this cry had won the critical elections of 1948 when the Nationalists came to power. That fear rested rightly or wrongly on the supposition still much prevalent in the early 1990s that two major ethnic groups could not share political power. Not only was this seen to be unworkable, but it threatened white and especially Afrikaner identity, and was therefore intolerable.

Through these years as Afrikaners began to see clearly into the future, it became increasingly difficult for them to contemplate unwinding conquest after 350 years of struggling to secure it. And the fears of doing this were becoming pathological as the decade of the 1990s got under way. Right-wingers had a political field day exploiting these fears.

On the black side, political fear took the form of a huge anxiety that the reform process might suddenly unravel and that the liberation and revolutionary struggle would have to go back almost to square one in order to triumph.

Second there was sheer, naked, cold-blooded *physical fear* in many hearts. This was especially true in the townships where both criminal and political violence held deadly sway both day and night. The statistics through these times were awesomely terrible. For example, in the first four months of 1992 serious crimes went up by 35,000 compared with 1991. The police force of 97,000 members had to deal with 145,000 cases of crime per month. There were 120 more murders per month than the previous year, thus bringing the total number of murders for 1992 up to 15,000. There were 61,000 people out on bail for crimes of various levels of seriousness, and statisticians delighted to inform us that in the 20 years from 1972 to 1992, crime had gone up by 1,000 per cent. By early 1993 South Africa could boast 77 murders a day of one sort or another.

Danger of Civil War

Then there was the ever-intensifying rivalry between the ANC and the Inkatha Freedom Party, and between the ANC and other homeland groupings and governments.

IFP anger stemmed from feelings of being marginalised and insulted in the political process. They were thus trying to make their presence felt.

On the other side were activists who saw chaos and violence as stepping stones on the way to a new order. One journalist in October 1992 put his lament this way: 'We have people who seem determined that the theories of Marx and Lenin should be given just one last whirl – two-stage revolution, centralised political control and a command economy. And we have the ingredients of civil war – heavily armed groups, territories, no-go zones, extreme intolerance, tit-for-tat atrocities and a win-at-all-costs mentality.'

Looking at Angola and Mozambique, the journalist added: 'Neither country set out to fight a civil war. It just happened, the way armed groups now clash in the streets of South Africa and communities live in terror. It starts as a gentle enough slope, but is extremely slippery and it soon steepens.' Douglas Hurd, British Foreign Secretary, visiting South Africa commented: 'South Africa is on a slide.' One black political leader commented: 'We must get used to the smell of blood.'

And so the prognosis was frightening. Not only did the negotiating process seem to be in peril, but the society seemed to be slipping into ungovernability.

An Ungovernable Society

One of the problems was that the liberation movements had in many ways preached that the country needed to be made ungovernable. This revolutionary vision remained deeply imbedded in the psyche of the so-called 'lost generation' of black youngsters in the townships. *Sunday Times* editor Ken Owen, writing on 8 May 1993, observed:

The danger is greatly magnified by the visible ebbing of the power of the government to govern. Faced with rampaging mobs, the police and armed forces have the choice of doing nothing or of responding with the sort of violence that must unleash even greater forces of destruction. The point has passed where black people can be beaten back into submission except by the use of force on a barbarous scale. Yet the Nationalist leaders, goaded by their own evident impotence, are retreating into the rhetoric, empty but provocative, of suppression by force. They threaten, bluster and warn.

Owen concluded his editorial saying:

Two sets of leaders, neither side entirely sure it can restrain its own followers, have brought their legions face to face, in conditions of rising tension, where any reckless or foolish act may set the dry tinder alight. To think that this situation can continue without tragedy is to strain the mercy of heaven.

Letters to the press showed the strident and desperate anxiety, particularly of frightened and sometimes reactionary whites. Yet what they were seeing did indeed often give grounds for despair. Said one letter:

The new South Africa which is upon us is nothing but a chaotic, lawless mess. Law and order is not maintained as rampaging mobs take over our cities. It is not the fault of the police: their hands are being tied by the whining liberals who never cease pointing fingers at the police, but who hardly raise a whimper of protest against the Marxist instigators of the violence and their ecclesiastical henchmen.

It was hard for church leaders to face this kind of accusation in these dreadful and difficult years. But accusations and counter-accusations flew fast and furiously in all directions.

They were tough days, make no mistake.

Economic Woes

On top of all this there was a profound sense in the country of our economy nosediving. Jumbo jet tourist flights were cancelled or turned back after the assassination of Chris Hani. Our economic growth rate was down to zero or even negative at times. Unemployment stood at 51 per cent of the potential working force and it was up to 80 per cent in some of the townships. As many as 1,600 people a day were entering the job market, most of them with little chance of securing employment. Only seven in every hundred school-leavers, we were told, would find jobs in the formal, industrial and commercial sectors. I remember chatting to the head of medical affairs in Natal who told me that they had been required to implement a budget cut of R20 million which would mean 500,000 patients being turned away from hospitals in our province the following year.

Then there was the housing shortage which haunted the nation, calling for over six hundred houses per day to be built in order to meet the two-million-unit shortfall.

On the educational front, we were told that 25 per cent of blacks had no formal education and 50 per cent were functionally illiterate. Out of every 100,000 blacks entering school, only one was destined to get an adequate pass at university level. In fact only 7 per cent of the total population was getting any higher education at all.

What was to become of us? That was the question in everybody's hearts.

Many whites coped simply by leaving the country. Jennifer Langford who works at Jan Smuts Airport said: 'A blanket of heaviness and the feeling of being abandoned overcame us each evening as we saw our planes filling up night after night with people leaving the country.

The vast majority of blacks, who could not contemplate anything like that, just got more angry.

The wood in the tinder box was getting dryer and seemed to be just waiting for a match.

But there was more.

Constitutional Impasse

Part of the problem was, of course, that there really seemed to be no final and clear way out of our constitutional impasse and political logjam. Our problems seemed to be insoluble and agreement totally elusive as to whether a unitary or federal state could provide the way through. While the ANC and others called for a unitary state with centralised powers, the IFP and other groups called for a federal structure, believing that in a heterogeneous nation South Africa would find a solution only in the federal direction. They affirmed that in resisting this, their political antagonists were flying in the face of all the nationalistic and ethnic movements of the world and seemingly the lessons of Eastern Europe and the former Soviet Union.

As an international backdrop to all of this, the Bosnian war raged as Yugoslavia came apart at the seams.

One British writer, John Alison, pressed upon us the comparison in an awesome warning. He wrote:

All I can say is this, Yugoslavia, an artificial, post-World War I construction, has far more homogeneity than South Africa. The Serbs, Croats, Slovenes and Islamic Bosnians are all of Slav stock and all speak Slavonic. Modern history has proved one thing clearly – that each of these related nations is prepared to spill its blood to secure independence.

What we have witnessed in Yugoslavia is a foretaste

of things to come in South Africa – unless they change course while there is time.

The differences in race, colour, religion, language and culture in South Africa are far more marked than in Yugoslavia.

That South Africa will break up is inevitable: it is merely a question of when and how.

Was that really the destiny to which we were doomed? I did not believe it had to be the case. Not if dialogue and understanding could prevail.

GLIMMER OF HOPE

So there was some light, albeit faint, at the end of the tunnel. But for me it was based less on our mental toughness and deal-making capabilities than on the spirit of prayer which was developing in our nation through those years.

Everywhere one turned, there were vigils or chains of prayer. Individuals, groups and whole congregations were praying across the land from east to west and north to south.

But even so, every one of us knew, the presence and power of God notwithstanding, that we remained a nation on a knife-edge.

3 From Africa with Love

Ex Africa Semper Aliquid Novi
(Out of Africa Always Something New)

Pliny

Milton Obote's soldiers came and shot my daughter and son-in-law. But we had to forgive and in the power of Christ were able to do so.

Bishop Yohana Mukasa of Uganda

In the situation in which South Africa found itself in the early 1990s, all concerned people knew they had to knuckle down and do their bit. While God was still in the business of Dunkirk-type miracles, nevertheless every person had to play a part under Him and put to sea, whether with yacht, motor boat, canoe or dinghy.

So it was that politicians, business people, sportsmen and women, academics, churchmen and women, and Christian leaders all put in their oar to keep the Lord's miraculous rescue process on the go.

But at times even this seemed not enough. The townships continued to boil, violence escalated, and when Los Angeles blew on 1 May 1992 in the rioting aftermath of police brutality on African-American Rodney King, the ANC's Natal Midlands leader Harry Gwala thundered: 'We are quite capable of reproducing the Los Angeles scenes here in Pietermaritzburg.' And indeed scenes not unlike those in Los Angeles were common in townships and cities around the nation.

AFRICAN PROBLEM

However, if our fortunes were to be restored with the Lord's help, it also seemed necessary to get some human help. And not just from anywhere. We needed help from Africa. For South Africa is part of a very large piece of real estate called Africa, and this means that ours is an African problem needing African insights from the wider African experience.

As it happened, 1992 was the thirtieth anniversary of African Enterprise's first citywide Christian mission. A celebratory week was held in Pietermaritzburg in August and a number of colleagues from our East and Central African evangelistic teams were invited to share in this experience. We called the venture Harambee '92, 'harambee' being the Swahili word for 'pulling together'. And never had there been such a need in South Africa for the spirit of everyone pulling together than at that time. However, while hoping and praying that many of our associates would be able to join us for a localised effort in Pietermaritzburg, we suddenly became convinced four weeks before the exercise opened that we should issue a Macedonian Call[1] to our colleagues to help us with a ministry of encouragement to the people of South Africa generally and to its leaders particularly.

While many others were involved in various efforts, this was the little slice of action which we felt we should take on as an act of obedience to what seemed to be God's guidance to us at that time. This was our little Dunkirk dinghy headed for. South Africa's beaches of political peril, alienation and despair.

And of course it made some real sense. After all, our colleagues from Kenya, Uganda, Ethiopia, Rwanda, Tanzania, Malawi and Zimbabwe had all been through the transition from colonial to majority rule and could undoubtedly share various lessons from these experiences.

Second, they knew first-hand that it was not appropriate for us in South Africa to have Utopian expectations of so-called majority rule. If anybody knew, they did, that 'Uhuru' was not a panacea for all ills, least of all if God and the spiritual side of things are left out of the picture.

Third, our colleagues were in a fine position to warn about the dangers of allowing violence to become endemic. For example, in Uganda, 800,000 people had died through tribal and political violence.

Fourth, in several of their countries they had seen economies shattered and could likewise warn against the dangerous social and political consequences of allowing a nation's economy to be ruined in the process of trying to fix things politically.

Finally, and perhaps above all, our colleagues had come out of a context of spiritual revival which had been going on for more than fifty years and which had been most notably characterised by the spirit of Calvary love and forgiveness so desperately needed in South Africa.

Wow!

One of the happiest, most memorable and in a sense proudest days in many years was 10 August 1992. My heart took wings as I met our colleagues at Durban Airport. Most of them had waited years to visit this land midst all its tensions, traumas and possibilities. Two things I will never forget about the drive back to Pietermaritzburg. First, I found in my heart a strange sense of poignant and wistful pride about South Africa, in spite of the horror of its policies. Here was a land of extraordinary beauty, amazing people and staggering potential. And besides, the country, warts and all, was mine. And I loved it.

The second and specially memorable dimension of that drive was that the whole way I heard nothing but 'Wow!'

from members of the party as they observed the hugely developed nature of South Africa relative to the rest of the continent. 'This is the kind of development all of Africa has been struggling and even fighting to achieve, and here you have it all in place. We pray you people will not throw it all away by descending into violence or civil war as has happened in other African countries.'

In many ways during that drive, I saw South Africa with new eyes because I was seeing it through the admiring eyes of East and Central Africans who, while they obviously hated apartheid and all its works, nevertheless could recognise something very special in what we have here.

From Africa with Love

Our colleagues, along with a healthy component of South Africans, set out in seven teams around the country on their ministry tour of testimony and encouragement. They went to every sector from radicalised township youth, to schools and colleges, and to business, military, police, political and professional leadership. They took a total of 201 meetings in the space of a fortnight. This provided a comprehensive overview of what was going on around the country, what people were thinking and how they were reacting, not only to the South African situation in general, but to the sorts of things coming to them from the East and Central Africans. Thus, the experiences of this tour provided a good barometer of the socio-political and spiritual climate in South Africa during the latter part of 1992.

Eastern Cape

Emmanuel Kopwe of Tanzania and his team went to East London on 26 August where they met with ANC leadership. Great bitterness was expressed about the situation in the Ciskei whose leader, Brigadier Oupa Gqozo, had recently withdrawn from the National Peace Accord. A very serious bone of contention was the existence in Ciskei of what was known as 'Section 43', a law which required permission from a magistrate for a meeting of even twenty people. The ANC leaders professed to have evidence that Brigadier Gqozo had instructed his magistrates to refuse this permission if it were applied for by ANC people.

The ANC leaders then told Emmanuel and his party, as well as Angus Robinson, who had arranged the meeting, that the Regional Peace Structure of the National Peace Accord was clearly not working. But they appealed to our folk and the Peace Accord representatives to do what they could.

The group asked Emmanuel whether he would try to play some kind of intermediary role between Brigadier Gqozo and themselves. 'We need to talk for the sake of peace.' Emmanuel felt totally daunted. Who wouldn't?

The next day Emmanuel and Angus went up to Bisho, capital of the Ciskei, to meet with Brigadier Gqozo. Minutes before entering the meeting, Gqozo had arrived from Durban where he had just given an address. It had gone very badly and Gqozo was feeling depressed. Having no brief for Ciskei politics generally or Gqozo specifically, Emmanuel said he nevertheless felt sorry for him. 'He had been deeply wounded by a remark made at the meeting, where he was "mud-slung" by some there, one of whom stood up and said: "How can we have this dog speak here at this meeting?"

'I may not go with his politics,' said Emmanuel, 'but that is a very terrible thing to say to a person and it is a great blow to anyone's humanity.' In apparent trauma and depression Gqozo then said: 'The ANC hate me because they know I will never accept their policy of socialism. So they want me removed. I have tried to reason with them but they are not interested and all they want is my removal.' But Emmanuel remembered how the ANC leadership, for their part, had spoken of the intransigence of Gqozo, his strong-arm tactics with opposition and his distancing of himself from the National Peace Accord. Others said he was 'a butcher'.

Tanzanian Emmanuel was not to know where truth really lay. But the general rhetoric was not helping a situation which was threatening to plunge the whole area into catastrophe.

'I kept praying for wisdom from the Lord,' said Emmanuel later. 'It was so hard to know what to do, but I said to Gqozo that, as he was a professing Christian, he should meet on a personal level with members of the ANC leadership, some of whom also professed to be Christians. They should try and speak together as children of God rather than as political opponents. I encouraged Gqozo to try and walk the Jesus Way because when Jesus was threatened He did not respond with violence. Jesus should be allowed to reign in the situation and people on different sides of the struggle should never stop looking to Him for reconciliation.'

Emmanuel was quite touched when Gqozo said that he had much appreciated the counsel and that the meeting had brought 'some healing oil on my spirit'.

Later that day our office received a fax from Angus saying: 'Today's East London *Daily Dispatch* reports that there will be an ANC march on Bisho, capital of the Ciskei, on September 9th. I believe Emmanuel would defuse the situation if he returns to East London in early September. Could you consider and pray about this?'

Having been invited not only by local Christians but by the ANC and Brigadier Gqozo himself, Emmanuel seemed well placed to do something. The Peace Accord representatives were very concerned and were also headed to the Eastern Cape. They would make contact with Emmanuel and the effort would be mounted together.

Not being a local yokel, and knowing local peace-makers were also involved in the exercise, Emmanuel felt he should wait to be contacted from the Peace Accord side. Something must have gone wrong, and to this day we don't know what it was. But Emmanuel sat waiting for the key telephone call which would link him with the Peace Accord exercise and take him back into the peacemaking process. With the call not coming and efforts to make contact with the major parties foundering, Emmanuel sat out the weekend in utter and total frustration and by Sunday night was ready to pop. His big concern was the ANC march which he felt could have disastrous consequences unless Gqozo and his militia, and indeed the ANC marchers themselves, worked out some proper ground rules for the exercise and began to understand one another's grievances. Having a good relationship with Gqozo and as a Tanzanian whom the ANC also respected, he obviously felt he could do something.

Emmanuel was distraught as the march moved forward relentlessly to take place a couple of days later. In the event it was a catastrophe. Shooting broke out as about 40,000 ANC protesters[2] marched on the capital, leaving 28 dead and around 200 wounded.[3] Columnist Allister Sparks wrote some days later:

> The Ciskei bloodbath signals one stark message: unless we can cut short the deadly spiral of political gamesmanship that our major organisations are engaged in, this country is doomed. We shall sink into a quagmire of internecine squabbling where the developed world will abandon us as just another no-hope basket case, to be sent occasional food aid when famine threatens, as in Somalia, but otherwise to be ignored and left to its own miseries. We are rushing towards that kind of disaster with the heedlessness of the Gadarene swine.

Thus endeth one little story which began with promise and ended with tragedy.

Ulundi

Going north was another team headed for Ulundi and a time with Chief Minister Mangosuthu Buthelezi, a maternal great-grandson of King Cetshwayo, and his colleagues in the leadership of the Inkatha Freedom Party.

The Ulundi plain, ringed by low, grass-covered hills, is about 220km north of Durban and about 90km inland from the coast. It was here in 1879 that the power of the Zulu nation under King Cetshwayo was finally broken by British troops under Lord Chelmsford, who then marched on Ondini, a few kilometres away, and burned the royal residence. It is an event which lives still in the Zulu memory as if yesterday.

We enjoyed a rewarding time of open discussion during which Chief Buthelezi expressed the feeling that only the churches could bring about the spirit of tolerance and sensitivity which was so desperately needed. He also denounced violence as the means to obtaining power, but acknowledged that fighting was going on.

At the end of the time we indicated that we would like to pray for him. At this point, to the astonishment of everyone, and especially the East Africans, he moved quickly into the centre of the room, and knelt down with his head bowed. All felt it was a humble and sincere act. The prayers that followed for the Chief, the country, the other parties, and for the whole negotiating process were intense and wrung from the heart.

Commented Emmanuel Kibira of Tanzania, and a close friend of former President Julius Nyerere: 'The meeting with Chief Buthelezi was quite different from all we had expected. I felt he was a Christian who is sincere and genuine and in the right spirit. He admitted that there were Inkatha elements which were out of control and that some of the violence had therefore become endemic and he deplored this.'

The team left Ulundi, thankful and excited about the day but pondering what would be the outcome of this great struggle between the IFP and the ANC. Could it be peacefully resolved, or would it end in the much-prophesied civil war which people were starting to talk about?

CAPITAL TIME

A few days later several of our teams were in Pretoria, the capital city. First port of call for one of these was with Dr Andries Treurnicht, leader of the right-wing Conservative Party, viewed throughout South Africa as a notorious white supremacist, the most eloquent and vocal advocate of a volkstaat and possibly the white man most hated by blacks throughout South Africa. I said to John Gatu of Kenya: 'There is probably not a single black man in South Africa who is willing to do what you are doing today in visiting this man.'

Gatu raised his eyebrows and smiled his warm Kikuyu smile, as if to say: 'That's no problem with me.'

Once seated round the table and served with characteristically strong Afrikaner coffee, Dr Treurnicht, who welcomed us warmly, told us something about his party's policies. Once a minister in the Dutch Reformed Church, and a former newspaper editor in Pretoria, he said that his deep desire had been to apply the principles of the Bible to practical, social and political life. This, he said, was not always easy because in politics the name of the game is power, not the power of God's Spirit, but the power of man who is a sinner. As such, man will always want to dominate others around him.

Treurnicht noted that South Africa has a great variety of communities and the question was how to formulate a model in which there existed understanding and co-operation between groups of people without the danger of one group's dominating another based on man's sinful power lusts. He said he believed that a system could be found which excluded the possibility of one community's dominating the others but to find this 'will take time, patience and much prayer, as well as humility and wisdom'. Testimonies of God working in lives and countries in the spirit of forgiveness were then brought by Bishop Gresford Chitemo of Tanzania and by John Gatu. Treurnicht listened fascinated, his eyes almost popping out of his head. Bishop Chitemo, a man of enormous Christian compassion, touched the Conservative leader when he said: 'Jesus Christ has changed my life and made me see that every person is precious in His sight. When I committed my life to Him, anger and hatred disappeared and I have a great hope that God is going to do the same thing in South Africa. We are praying for you, Dr Treurnicht, that God will grant you wisdom, understanding and knowledge of how this country should be governed in future.'

Treurnicht seemed moved by the ingenuous and simple sincerity of this gracious Tanzanian. But John Gatu brought the emotional uppercut which impacted all of us.

He told Dr Treurnicht that years previously he had been caught up in the Mau Mau movement and had hated whites with a passion. But then he had been converted to Christ. His heart began to change and this hatred diminished dramatically. But he still felt 'a residual bitterness towards Afrikaners in general, and the Conservative Party in particular, and towards you, Dr Treurnicht, even more particularly'.

Treurnicht looked wide-eyed, wondering what on earth was coming next.

Then humbly and slowly, his eyes riveted on Treurnicht's, Gatu went on: 'But meeting you here today and sensing in you a warm human being who wants to follow the Lord, I have to say to you that, although I do not agree with your politics at all, or some of your interpretations of the Bible, the Spirit of God is convicting me of my attitude towards you and I want to ask for your forgiveness. While I may not like someone's views, my Bible does not allow me to be bitter towards that person. I therefore want to give you the right hand of fellowship and greet you as my brother.'

At this he stood and held out his right hand to grasp the hesitating hand of Dr Treurnicht, whose previously startled eyes were now filled with tears.

'Nothing like this has ever happened to me before' said Treurnicht. 'And certainly no black man has ever called me brother before.'

As we stepped out into the sunlight of a cheerful Pretoria street lined with its legendary jacarandas, I reflected upon the almost mysterious wistfulness evident in this political mystery man. Did he feel in those moments some elemental twinges of remorse that his prejudice had perhaps overcome his piety and that his Afrikaner nationalism had overcome his sense of humanity?

But I will never be privy to what, if anything, he felt. A matter of months later Dr Treurnicht was dead from a violent heart attack. I often wonder where he and others like him might have ended up, had they been loved long beforehand by forgiving black men such as John Gatu.

Union Buildings

The next day, Thursday, 3 September, our team went to the Union Buildings to meet President F.W. de Klerk.

As we were seated, de Klerk turned to me and whispered: 'We should open in prayer.' It was the natural and spontaneous suggestion of a man who obviously knew what dependence on God was all about. Bishop Chitemo of Tanzania led us most beautifully. Following the President's sincere words of personal welcome he opened the way for us to bring our message.

Edward Muhima, our team leader in Uganda, smiled warmly at de Klerk and said: 'Mr President, we do thank God for the kind of man you are and for what you have achieved here in South Africa. Indeed we believe that you could be the Moses of Africa.' It was one of those bold statements which almost takes one's breath away. Then Edward went on: 'But, Mr President, I would remind you that in order for Moses to lead the Children of Israel out of Egypt, he had to leave the courts of Pharaoh.'

I wasn't quite sure if Edward fully appreciated the gravity of what he was saying, but sensed that there was perhaps here an unwitting prophecy of both the privilege and the price of the kind of liberating leadership which de Klerk had brought to the Presidency of South Africa.

The discussion continued for well over an hour, at the end of which de Klerk spoke most movingly of how the need for fundamental change had grown deeply in his heart. He concluded: 'What our country needs is real reconciliation, not a Hollywood-type of reconciliation but one which goes right to the heart of man. That is why I need, and have been blessed by, the prayers of so many people. This means so much in terms of what I am trying to do.'

The man's sense of genuine sincerity shone through as he spoke. As I looked round the room, my colleagues were riveted.

'And I do feel that these prayers really strengthen me,' he went on, 'and your visit and the spirit in which we are able to meet have given me courage at a time when I am feeling discouraged.'

He was referring to the decision of the ANC a couple of days previously not to resume further negotiations with the government. Thankfully the ANC later agreed to continue these negotiations.

'That is a great man,' said Bishop Yohana Mbogori of Kenya as we left the Union Buildings.

Shell House

Unfortunately when we visited Shell House next day for our appointment with some of the ANC executive, Nelson

Mandela was caught up on an emergency assignment and so could not be with us. But their delegation of ten or so was led by the gracious President of the ANC, Oliver Tambo, who had suffered a stroke some months previously. 'I used to be the one who had lots to say,' he commented with a smile, 'but now it is not possible for me to say much. So I must let others speak for us.' As he was about to get the proceedings under way, however, George Wanjau, Presbyterian leader from East Africa, commented daringly with a chuckle, 'Brother Tambo, yesterday when we were with Mr de Klerk, he felt we should open with prayer. I hope the ANC does not think we can dispense with prayer!' There was huge laughter, to which Mr Tambo responded: 'No, of course we must open with prayer. Please lead us.'

After an encouraging time of sharing, Mr Tambo was particularly touched when several of us gathered round him to pray for his health. His partial paralysis and struggles with speech tugged poignantly at one's heartstrings. 'A gentleman,' I thought. 'Yes, a real gentleman.' And what struggles, heartache and pain he had experienced over all the years of loneliness in exile while South Africa propelled itself on the momentum of political madness rather than racial reconciliation and justice.

Later as we got out into the street below Shell House, Edward Muhima spotted several fiery looking young lads sporting Mkhonto'weSizwe T-shirts. They were looking at our group very curiously, especially the few with dog collars, as if these were some sort of aliens from outer space. One of them asked Edward why our group was there and whom we were seeing. After Edward explained, they responded that they were from the combat section of the ANC. 'Tell me more about that,' asked Edward with genuine interest.

'We will get to power by force of arms and after that we will rule,' said one of them emphatically.

Edward smiled at the speaker, and then lovingly but firmly responded: 'Well, we have come from other parts of

Africa to encourage you people to move forward through the processes of negotiation, because it is better to solve problems by talking than with the barrel of a gun. That's what we have found in Uganda.'

One of the lads retorted: 'But there are certain people who do not understand any language other than the language of the gun.'

'Maybe,' replied Edward, 'but supposing you overthrow them with the gun, won't they use the same gun to overthrow you? How then will there be an end to the crisis?'

'What do you suggest?' asked one of the youths, seemingly intrigued by Edward's sincerity and firmness.

'I encourage you to negotiate,' said the Ugandan, 'and I believe that negotiations between the government and the ANC and all the other movements must go forward. You must iron out your differences and capitalise on the things which unite you. Otherwise you could end up going the way of Uganda where we lost 800,000 people because we began fighting.'

The youths looked pensive and then one of them said: 'It's true we need peace and we know peace can only come by negotiation. But at the same time, if we are going to make our arguments strong, we must have the backing of the gun.'

At this moment our kombi drew up and the somewhat perplexed youths drifted towards the door of Shell House as Edward called back to them: 'Don't forget, young friends, that if you remove people by the gun, they will use that same gun to remove you.'

PAC

I think this conversation got Edward's blood running strongly because he was again quite vigorous in conversation as we met with half a dozen or so of the executive of the Pan Africanist Congress led by their legendary Secretary General, Benny Alexander.[4]

Benny underlined the PAC's belief that there could one day be a United States of Africa, echoing the vision five decades ago of Kwame Nkrumah of Ghana. 'There could even be a Pan African army which could look after Africa's interests and command the respect of the world.'

'Isn't that a bit unrealistic?' asked one of our group.

'No,' said Benny, 'not if you believe in the power and reality of dreams coming true. One must dream. Our founder Robert Sobukwe dreamed and only by this kind of vision can Africa generally and South Africa particularly find its feet and shake off the shackles of racism and stand tall in the world.'

'And what about your slogan, "one settler, one bullet"?' asked Edward.

'Oh, that's hangover language from the war days and is just a psychological ploy to frighten the enemy.'

But Edward was not to be fobbed off: 'My brothers,' he said, 'I think that is very dangerous. If you people at the top as leaders see the slogan "one settler, one bullet" as just a psychological ploy to scare the enemy, there is no way that your young people on the ground or your military operatives can understand it that way. They will take it literally. That is something you must really work on changing.'

Sharpeville

While these and other visits to political leadership were going on, different teams were ministering elsewhere.

In Sharpeville, scene of course of the infamous 1960 massacre, the team visited the former home of a family who a few months previously had lost no less than seven members in one attack. Only one nineteen-year-old girl survived.

'I'll tell you what happened here,' said our guide, Dr Kolokoto of the South African Council of Churches, 'and I will tell you how this young woman survived. As the rest of her family were mowed down, this girl, covered in the blood of other members of her family after the shooting, but otherwise unhurt herself, had fallen down among the dead bodies and pretended to be dead herself. She later extricated herself from among the bodies of her family, in the midst of whom and in whose blood she had lain for some time in utter devastation and trauma before she went for help.' The team was told by a distant family member, who now lives in the house, that the terrified young woman was still in hiding, fearing the return of the killers.

'This is the kind of thing our African pastors in these townships are dealing with every day,' said Dr Kolokoto. 'And how can this kind of thing ever be healed or come right except by the power of the Gospel?'

Bishop Yohana Mukasa of Uganda knew this and testified: 'Milton Obote's soldiers came and shot my daughter and son-in-law. But we had to forgive, and in the power of Christ were able to do so.'

CLOSING WEEKEND

As the closing weekend, 5 and 6 September, arrived, our various teams converged on Johannesburg, all of them on a high and full of reports about their various experiences and encounters all around the country.

Kenyans Gershon and Gladys Mwiti had had an extraordinary time in Cape Town. Dan Serwanga of Kenya, Berhanu Deresse of Ethiopia and Harry Mkombwe of Zimbabwe had been fascinated by their encounter with dynamic Trevor Evans, Managing Director of NAMPAC, who had called his top management together to meet our team and reflect on how business should move proactively into the future.

Edward Muhima had a touching end to his time in Johannesburg. Early in the morning in the home in which he was staying, the young eight-year-old son of his white host and hostess came into his bedroom and said: 'Oh,

Uncle Edward, why are you going away? I'm going to miss you when you go.' At which the lad burst into tears.

'To me,' reported Edward afterwards, 'that was the most touching word from a little white boy as he called a black man his uncle and said he would miss me. And when he began to weep, I also broke down. Later when I was saying goodbye to his mother, father and sister, we all burst into tears. It is an indication that something is happening when such feelings can be expressed between black and white people.'

So greatly did this experience impact Edward that later in the morning, when he preached in the Florida Methodist Church, he came down from the pulpit and called two children to come to him. Picking them up in his arms he said: 'If for no other reason than for the sake of these young children, I urge all of you in South Africa, whites and blacks, to reconcile. Otherwise you will bequeath to these children a terrible world.'

As it transpired, the two children came from a very conservative family and the two parents, who were present at the service, were greatly moved by this simple act.

'From Africa with Love' was coming to a close. I have told only a few of the many stories of a nation struggling to burst out of the prison of its past and find its way into the future.

But what struck me, particularly after the meetings with political leadership, was how close at one level and in general terms all of these different leaders and groupings were to each other. All spoke of a new South Africa with justice, harmony, reconciliation, democracy and a sound economy. Virtually all embraced an appreciation of God and all needed and appreciated prayer. But sectional and group interests, the past legacy of mistrust, and the tyranny of the constituency were keeping each group from doing the really statesmanlike thing in finding a meaningful way to a solution for the nation. Among the high-calibre leaders we had met, there was clearly enough political savvy, intellectual ability and moral strength to guide the nation into a solution acceptable to all and adequate to safeguard our future.

'Get Away and Talk'

But what if one could play a little part in helping some of these leaders to understand these realities more fully and their own relative closeness to one another?

What about, we thought, an open letter along these lines sent to all the senior leaders and published in the press? The penultimate paragraph included this little exhortation:

'Why not go to the bush, climb the Drakensberg, hide in a hotel, go anywhere, but just get away and talk? Just find each other.' Yes, it was a sound idea.

But now came a new thought. What about helping such a thing to happen? Even for just a few leaders? After all, every little bit could help.

4 Kolobe Kaleidoscope

Hear the other side.

St Augustine

I know a place called Kolobe.

Rupert Lorimer

I learned more in my first three hours at Kolobe than I could have learned in six years anywhere else.

Lekau Moyaha (AZAPO)

Johannesburg's Jan Smuts Airport, with all of its sounding gongs and clanging cymbals, as St Paul would have put it, is not the best place for creative conversations. But I won't quickly forget my chat there with Rupert Lorimer over a cup of coffee on Friday, 9 October 1992.

Rupert was a longtime Democratic Party Member of Parliament. A man with a great heart for justice and racial reconciliation, he was profoundly involved not only in the parliamentary arena but in the Peace Accord endeavours in the Pretoria, Witwatersrand, Vereeniging (PWV) area (now known at 'Gauteng'). It seemed he would be a good person with whom to share our ideas developing out of the 'From Africa With Love' experiences.

'Rupert,' I said, midst endless interruptions from the sounding gongs, 'we've seen that so many of these political leaders are closer to each other than they realise. What about trying to get some of them together for a day –

maybe beginning with second-tier leadership – and help them to discover one another in real relationships? What do you think?'

Rupert's spontaneous enthusiasm for the idea startled me. 'Absolutely smashing thought,' he said with a grin lighting up his face. 'But a day is way too little. We need a weekend. And I know a place called Kolobe which would exactly fit the bill. It's a game lodge north of Pretoria, a super spot with facilities and cuisine appropriate for leaders – totally secluded and private with no security problems. Shall I check the availability?'

'By all means,' I said, a surge of excitement laying hold of my spirit. 'And let's do it soon! There's no time to waste, you know. We'll try and raise some money for it overseas. And we can think together about people to invite.'

I thereupon headed straight into town, first to the ANC and then to the PAC offices, to share the idea. Warm openness in both places suggested we were on track. The Kolobe dialogue weekends were under way.

My assistant, Peter Kerton-Johnson, was a champion as he and Rupert now ran in the next weeks to make it all happen. Friends in London put up the not-inconsiderable money we needed. The Lord's lights had all gone green.

A fly on the wall at Lanseria Airport on the edge of Johannesburg would have witnessed an interesting human happening on the afternoon of Friday, 4 December 1992. Peter, myself and George Wanjau – who had flown down from Kenya to be a neutral, non-South African presence – were hovering around anxiously waiting for the arrival of the rest of the mysterious mix of political peril and possibility which we had assembled.

From Durban we had already collected three members of our party. Girja 'Sunny' Singh was a prominent ANC member in Natal and one of the major leaders in the Natal Indian Congress. Prince Vincent Zulu, from the Zulu royal household, was the KwaZulu government's

Deputy Minister of Education and Culture. Then there was Dr Johan Steenkamp, MP and Information Director of the National Party in Natal. Already quite a mix. They sat on airport benches conversing awkwardly. No sign of the others. It was getting late.

Suddenly a car pulled up. Out stepped Lesaoana Makhanda from the Pan Africanist Congress (PAC) National Executive and their former representative at the United Nations. He was warm, friendly, congenial and apologetic. We introduced him all round and I sensed Steenkamp stiffen a little. Not only were PAC the 'one settler, one bullet' people, but a couple of days previously a number of whites in a sports club in King William's Town had been blown up and others maimed by a bomb for which APLA (Azanian People's Liberation Army) operatives had claimed responsibility.

After more waiting, finally in strode a distinguished, solid and greying African gentleman who looked very much the part of the veteran politician. And he was. John Nkadimeng was a National Executive Committee member of both the ANC and the South African Communist Party (SACP). He looked tense, no doubt wondering what on earth he was doing there. He might well have asked.

We were now ready. The others would travel by car and meet us at Kolobe.

Excitement

As our plane raced down the runway into the setting sun and rose over the bushveld north of Johannesburg, the first sense of excitement began to overtake our little fellowship of strangers. This was fun. The rolling hills, valleys and bushland below had a haunting beauty. South Africa is like that. If its people don't grab you, its loveliness will.

'CP country down there – Treurnicht's stomping ground,' chuckled Sunny Singh peering down from his window.

Steenkamp laughed. The first signs of relaxation were in the air.

'Help me find this landing strip!' bellowed the pilot above the roar of the engines. 'It's somewhere down there. Must be close now.'

ANC, IFP, NP, PAC and SACP, all thinking that maybe we'd lost our way, suddenly had their minds most wonderfully concentrated on the same thing. A new experience, no doubt.

'There it is!' shouted someone enthusiastically. The letters 'KOLOBE', written with white stones just visible in the dwindling light, stood out at the end of the little dust runway cut from the bush. The pilot flew exhilaratingly low to see if any stray rhino or hippo might be competing with us for space, then turned the plane's nose in and put her down with a flurry of flying dust and furious braking. I saw John Nkadimeng's face light up with the excitement of a schoolboy. Although he was in his sixties, it was his first ever experience of the bush. Not surprising if you've spent half your life in prison or exile.

The whole group were really beginning to enjoy themselves. The process was working.

The lights of two Land Rovers came into view. Game rangers Peter Morrison and Rod Stokes, khaki-uniformed with green epaulettes, introduced themselves and bundled us into the Rovers. The adventure was on. Vincent Zulu was beaming.

'What's that?' shouted Sunny as a Kudu bull, dramatic horns and all, scampered away from the track along which we were bumping and winding. A symphony of insect sounds now filled the air with music. It was the bush beckoning.

Strange feeling. A sense of common humanity began ever so imperceptibly to lay its happy clutches upon our spirits. We were becoming real people with and to each other and not just 'political positions' or 'postures'.

The moon came up. An owl flapped low over us. Magic

was at work. By the time the twinkling lights of the lodge were visible through the trees, the first inklings of what the new South Africa could be like had already begun to sink into of our perceptions. In the homey comfort of the thatched lounge Rupert Lorimer, Democratic Party MP, met us, looking for all the world like Alice in Wonderland's Cheshire Cat. His beam revealed a man saying 'Now, this is the life.' More than that, things he too had dreamed about were happening. He guided willing takers through to the pub while others found their rooms and unpacked.

Then dinner out in the 'boma', an open, under-the-stars enclosure hedged in by a circular bamboo and reed fence. A long lavishly furnished, candle-lit table occupied centre stage while a log fire crackled away on one side and on the other, under a thatched gazebo, an open carvery of meat and luscious vegetables beckoned.

'Do you think we could have a little NP-ANC rapprochment?' asked Johan Steenkamp as he sat down next to the now constantly chortling Nkadimeng. 'That's fine,' said Nkadimeng, 'provided we can find sufficient consensus on which wine to choose!'

As our meal got under way, conversation became more and more animated as ribbing, laughter and banter filled the air.

'Are these people really all from different political parties?' whispered game ranger Rod in my ear.

'You bet,' I replied as he shook his head in disbelief.

After dinner I told the group a bit about the origins of the exercise and how we had come to believe that an experiment in building relationships and trust across political barriers had seemed worth trying. Rupert shared how we'd hit on Kolobe where he had come many times for relaxation or environmental seminars.

Our weekend would have three components. We would each tell our stories and autobiographies. We would each share our vision of the new South Africa. And we would each explain the steps required, as we saw them, to reach the new South Africa. In between we would have a thundering good time, eat well, get some rest, go on game drives and picnics and maybe have a swim or two. Oh yes – and we would begin and end each day with devotions and prayer, just to remind ourselves that, like South Africa, we needed God if we were to come through properly.

At which I led the group in a little word of prayer that the Lord would bless us and give us a good time. And the day was over.

MYTHS EXPLODE

As some sat round the fire, others repaired to sample the wares of the pub and yet others sat down to watch the late TV news together, I headed off to my rondavel, a partitioned structure with two *en suite* bedrooms and a small lounge. I heard Lesaoana Makhanda's voice at what sounded like full pitch.

Thinking that he had perhaps already got into an almost violent political altercation with someone over the recent PAC bombings in King William's Town, I ventured to slide open his concertina door in the spirit of the Irishman who said: 'Is this a private fight, or may I join it?'

To my astonishment and slight embarrassment I realised I had intruded on the man's prayer time. He was calling on God, aloud, to intervene and save South Africa. I quickly tried to excuse myself with a rapid-fire apology.

'No, come on in, brother,' he called out. 'I was just talking to the Lord at the end of this amazing day.'

I was staggered. Was this a PAC man? A 'one settler, one bullet' fellow? My stereotype took an instant beating. Some mythology within me exploded.

As we talked, I was at length emboldened to ask: 'Brother, what about this bombing and these deaths in King William's Town? How does this fit with your faith and your prayers?'

'It's like this,' he replied. 'In the old days of the armed

struggle, our political and military operatives made decisions together and agreed on policies and practices. After
the liberation movements were unbanned, our political
leaders returned to the country, but most of our APLA
military generals stayed out, though many young operatives were still in the country. Then, without consulting
us political leaders, our operatives went ahead and these
things started to happen. We are very anxious about it.'

I could see now why the PAC's political leaders found
APLA violence as hard to denounce as they found it
embarrassing to approve. Hence Benny Alexander's
verbal gymnastics when questioned about this on TV.
However he answered he'd get it wrong with someone, possibly even those in his own party. So what do
you do?

At the end of the time of sharing, we prayed together,
agreed to share our time of devotions in the morning and
go for a run through the bush before breakfast. Which we
did. He in his best shoes and I barefoot!

'No lions or tigers here, brother,' I said. 'You can
relax!'

AZAPO

Saturday, 5 December dawned with a new feeling of
excitement and anticipation. After a magnificent breakfast, in the open air by the pool, the kind that gives
all weight-watchers withdrawal symptoms, we saw a car
pull up. Lekau Moyaha, a senior member of the Azanian
People's Organisation (AZAPO) Executive Committee,
plus a friend, had arrived from Pietersburg. The friend,
who looked as if he was also doubling as bodyguard, turned
out to be Selema Mashiane, Welfare Secretary for AZAPO
at the time.

They looked decidedly edgy. What had they got themselves into? As Lekau admitted later: 'We came very
suspicious of this whole thing. In fact, we came as spies

so we could report back to our Secretary General, who wanted us to help him decide whether he should accept to come next time. We were actually wondering if these whites wanted to murder us!'

And they seemed to have come prepared. Rod, the game ranger and former Selous Scout with Rhodesian Security in the bad old days, whispered to me just as we went into devotions: 'They have two AK47s under the seats of their car!'

At which point, just to thicken the plot, Chris de Jager, former senior colleague of Andries Treurnicht and now Deputy Leader of the AVU, turned up, also decidedly uncomfortable.

Could be quite a party, I thought.

PEACE

All were sitting in a circle under an open, thatch-roofed 'pondokkie' by the pool, when George Wanjau of Kenya began a short devotional time. He told of the Mau Mau experience of bitter animosity between blacks and whites and how the Christian spirit of forgiveness through Christ had had such an impact in winding down those animosities and bringing a spirit of reconciliation into the post-independence country.

'Even Jomo Kenyatta saw this and said on Independence Day, "We cannot build a new Kenya unless it be based on forgiveness. So you whites must forgive me for scaring you to death and I must forgive you for locking me up in prison!"' Added George: 'That's the way you've got to move in South Africa if you are to save this place. It's also the way for all of us this weekend.'

John Nkadimeng

Clearly the Kolobe experience had been working its spell, for warm and spontaneous conversation immediately followed. To my astonishment, John Nkadimeng, the communist and ANC Executive member, opened the batting, saying: 'Something is happening to me already. You see, we are breaking out of isolation. The fact is that the disease of ignorance breeds other very negative tendencies in society.'

He gave a big smile, as if to prepare some of us for a body blow. 'For myself I came out of a tribal background and because of what some white Christians did to us in the Northern Transvaal, I came to hate Christianity. Those people drove me to explore Karl Marx and I joined the South African Communist Party (SACP). But actually I was only a kitchen boy. In fact I told Braam Fisher in the Treason Trial of 1957,[1] when I was sentenced to two years in Kroonstad Prison, that I was a "kitchen boy" and he wouldn't believe it! But there you are, and now I am here with all of you and we are sharing different points of view. This is so good. And maybe we all need to be ready to abandon years in one posture if we feel that to be wrong. But we must be honest with each other. I must say I thank George for presenting his viewpoint to an old communist like me. You are very convincing, George. And I really didn't know there were Christians around like you people.'

I felt I had to respond to this.

'John, what you said about some Christians doing terrible things to you, and driving you into the arms of Karl Marx, really convicted me. I'd like for myself and on behalf of Christians to ask your forgiveness for that. It was very bad and we failed both you and our Lord.'

John smiled. 'This is wonderful. This kind of thing should be happening all over South Africa.'

Autobiographies

After tea, autobiography time was upon us. In all of the six Kolobe weekends which took place over the next year, the experience of hearing each other's autobiographies was the most magical and most transforming experience. For myths explode and stereotypes shatter. Humanity shines through. Mercy and compassion are born along with the desire to reach out and relate and accommodate. Observed Catherine the Great once: 'The more one knows, the more one forgives.'[2] This was our experience as we listened to one another.

Lesaoana

That morning Lesaoana Makhanda told us how he had completed his matric at a German Benedictine school. Said Makhanda, 'It was reported in a paper that Verwoerd's son, who took matric the same year I did, got a school leaving certificate and I achieved a university entrance. But I knew that, even though I had achieved this, I could not get into Wits University. This upset me terribly. So I got a bursary to study in Lesotho for the Catholic priesthood. But the government confiscated my passport which militated against my ever becoming a priest.

'In 1958 I began associating with some politicians within the ANC called "the Africanists", a group who wanted to form a new organisation that would address specifically the issue of land. That triggered something in me, because I understood what they were on about. Now I could begin to express some of the frustrations going on in my mind. So in 1959, I was one of the youngest delegates at the inaugural convention of the Pan Africanist Congress.

'In 1963, we undertook a mission to steal mortar bombs from the Voortrekkerhoogte military base. We had an enormous suitcase and managed to put about eighty of these small bombs in it. It was this that led to my arrest, along with thirty-one of my colleagues. Six of them were sentenced to life in prison.

'You know, I now have some friends in the South African Defence Force. And in October of 1993 I was invited for a meeting at the SADF headquarters in Pretoria with General Meiring and several other military officials. I mentioned to one of the colonels that I had once stolen bombs from the military base, but he was not amused at all!

'Anyway,' Lesaoana continued, 'our lawyer told us the case would be thrown out and we had better leave the country because we could be rearrested and charged again. So we devised a way to escape after the verdict. The judge told a packed courtroom the case had been withdrawn and the bailiff opened the gate for us to be escorted back to our cells. But before he knew what was happening, everyone was jumping around all over the place, deliberately creating pandemonium so we could make our escape. That was the last time I saw my parents.

'We secretly crossed into Botswana and then travelled to Tanzania with a group of SWAPO members. Conditions in Dar es Salaam were very tough, sleeping in a small, disused German airport with no roof over our heads. But at least we were free.'

After commando training in Egypt, Lesaoana and others came back to Tanzania where they were then arrested because of their disagreements with the liberation committee of the Organisation of African Unity (OAU) regarding the appropriate strategy to be employed for liberating South Africa.

'We were finally put in touch with an American missionary who knew of some South Africans in America who wanted people to come for scholarships.'

It was arranged by Tom Mboya and singer Miriam Makeba that Lesaoana and his colleagues could go to the United States for study at a university. 'Miriam sent us a hundred dollars each, but seeing we had been living in such awful conditions, we gave all the money to our friends in Dar es Salaam. We felt we were going to a rich country where there would be no need to have the money! But when we got to London, we were very scantily dressed and it was wintertime. We had nothing with us and we did not want people to think there was something wrong with us. So we took twenty-five-kilogram sacks and put soil in them so people would think we had real luggage and clothes!'

The next twenty-seven years of Makhanda's life were spent in the United States, working for Gulf Oil and later for the PAC at the UN. It was here that he came to faith through Zoë Ministries in New York. 'I had become discouraged with my Catholic church, even though I had nearly entered the priesthood. But one dark and wintry New York day, with the snow three or four feet deep, I was very depressed. Something out of the blue said to me: "Go into that church." So I went into a service at Doral Inn and met the Rev. Bernard Jordan, who prayed for me.

'In fact this pastor then "prophesied" over me and narrated to me my whole life, work and background without knowing anything about me at all. That is when I really found Jesus Christ and realised that God is there and He still speaks and the supernatural is real.'

'Well, I think that's about all,' said Lesaoana suddenly and anticlimactically as the rest of us caught our breath.

Sunny

'Bet you can't cap that?' said Peter to Sunny Singh.

'I doubt it,' said the ANC and Natal Indian Congress leader with a chuckle. 'That is really some story. Mine is less spectacular. I grew up in a very poor home. As I slowly saw the awful situation produced for our people by apartheid, I became politically aware and by the time the ANC formed Mkhonto' weSizwe in 1961, I was ready for it and got involved in 1962 in a series of actions around Durban. The upshot was that in 1963 I was sentenced to ten years for sabotage. I spent the first few weeks in a Johannesburg prison which was a frightening place. On arrival we were all asked to face the wall naked while guys in white coats came with buckets and soap to ram their fingers roughly into our rectums to see if we were bringing anything in.'

Sunny roared with laughter in recollection. 'But it was no joke, I assure you. And it was no Carlton Hotel. After showering in the early mornings we were not given any towels for drying off and had to try to get dry by running naked around the quad while hardened criminals chased us on the concrete surface. The white officer in charge battered one prisoner's back with a leather-covered cane. It was awful.'

Next came transfer to Robben Island with sixty-one others on the same truck, including Stanley Mogoba, now Presiding Bishop of the Methodist Church, and poet Dennis Brutus.

'After our arrival, people like Tsafendas, who assassinated Verwoerd, were brought in and locked up in isolation cells, where Nelson Mandela and others were confined. It was no picnic spot, I assure you,' he said chuckling.

In fact what struck all of us with Sunny was that he told his whole account midst constant gales of laughter and not a trace of bitterness.

We asked him about this. 'Well you know, you learned to laugh in prison. You either laughed or you cried. But you also had to develop inner strength because there was so much evil there. And it was awful how evil took over some of the warders. But we believed it was important to try and show a spirit of love and friendship, even to the warders and authorities.'

Sunny told how it was years before the awful boredom and tedium and hard labour were finally relieved by permission to study. 'I specialised in Russian and French literature with special attention on Tolstoy and Victor Hugo.

'Interestingly enough some of the junior warders were also taking correspondence courses and we even shared some of our books before exams which we then all wrote together in a big shelter, prisoners and warders alongside each other. And for a few brief moments we would forget we were meant to be enemies. But senior warders became very upset, even fearful, when they saw friendships develop between prisoners and junior warders and they would try to frustrate this. However in our common humanity, relationships of trust and confidence did in fact develop. And Mandela led the way in showing us we should have no bitterness.'

Sunny went on to tell how for eight years he was responsible for 'news' circulation among the prisoner. 'This was done on toilet rolls and I was caught as this and confined to the isolation cells many times. But it gave me an opportunity to communicate with the leadership and pass on the latest news I had. I remember when Albert Luthuli, the President of the ANC, was killed by a train in 1967, I broke the news to those confined in the isolation cells.

'The chief warder in those ten dark years was most brutal and sadistic. But we had to persevere and discipline our minds and hearts like a rock to withstand all of those brutalities. For me, the most memorable day on the Island was when I worked up the courage to approach the chief warder just before I and six of my comrades were going to be transferred to Johannesburg. We succeeded in having a very warm and humane discussion and I told him that we were not going to hold any grudges against him or any of his colleagues because they were also victims of apartheid in their own way. When I left him, he was almost in tears.'

Sunny was finally released in 1974 after ten years in prison. His spirit soared. His soul sang. His hopes began to revive.

'But all that was short-lived,' he added, 'because I was immediately placed for five years under house arrest. I eventually decided it was time to escape and, on Christmas Day 1976 at 2 a.m., I slipped across the border to Maputo in Mozambique where I worked for five years with John Nkadimeng before being expelled to Zambia for a year, then Holland where I was the ANC's representative for some time before coming back to South Africa a little while ago.

'So it's been a long business,' he concluded 'although I think South Africa is slowly coming right.' Then he turned reflective. 'But I am not too sure that, if I had not been in prison, whether I could have developed such a level of tolerance and, above all, humanity. I don't regret one bit that I spent ten years on the Island.

'Isn't it time for lunch?'

Sobered and challenged by this saga, we adjourned to savour Kolobe's cuisine, relax and get ready for the game drive that afternoon. Yes, this was richness. It was also life-changing. And for those of us who were white and had sent all the Lesaoanas and Sunnys of this world into those endless years of imprisonment and exile, their stories were shattering. What had we done?

It's a Rhino!

The game drive, ending in the gentle, late afternoon sun with a picnic tea in the bush, was pure magic. We were loaded up in two Land Rovers and our rangers drove us on separate tracks in different sections of the park for a couple of hours before a rendezvous by the river.

At one point our Land Rover came on a huge midden of rhino droppings. A midden, as Rod explained to us, is a kind of rhino toilet used to mark the various corners of his turf. It says to other mighty males, 'Beware all ye who enter here, for this territory is mine and the ladies are mine, too. So keep out, or thou knowest not what might happen to thee!'

Then suddenly the big beast himself was sighted about 40m away staring straight at us.

I wasn't of course present when Lot saw his wife turn into a pillar of salt, but John Nkadimeng's flabbergasted face would have competed well with Lot's. His eyes popped. But his face, momentarily frozen with fear, now burst into a radiant show of smiles and ecstatic delight.

'My goodness, look at that! It's amazing! A real, live rhino! I can't believe it! Won't he charge us? You know, I've never seen a rhino before. In fact I've never been in the bush like this before.'

He paused, then roared with laughter: 'And I've definitely never seen a midden before! You know, Nelson will never believe this. I need some evidence to prove where I've been and what I've seen.'

At this, he leaped from the Rover and picked up a huge, though thankfully old and dry, rhino pat – the size of a large grapefruit – and put it triumphantly at his feet in the rover while AVU, AZAPO, DP, IFP, NP, and PAC – not to mention AE! – really wondered if ANC would make a good government after all!

'I'm going to show this to Nelson on Monday when I report to him on the weekend,' grinned John.

My imagination, I must say, ran a little riot at that point as I imagined Nkadimeng in his boss's office on Monday, perhaps with other weighty worthies from the ANC Executive.

'Now, John,' I could hear Mandela saying, 'tell us about the Kolobe weekend. What was it like?'

And I could see Nkadimeng producing his huge rhino dropping and with arm militantly outstretched, making the awful announcement: 'It was like that!'

'My, oh my!' Mandela would say, recoiling in horror and reaching for his handkerchief. 'Was it that bad?'

Back at the lodge that evening and through the next day the stories continued, each one affecting every person in the group.

I remember Johan Steenkamp of the National Party exploding the idea that he was a settler, especially given that his forefather, Jan Steenkamp, had arrived at the Cape with Jan van Riebeeck in 1652! His mother's ancestors had come over in 1686.

'No sir, we are not settlers. We are part of Africa now and part of this soil. And we had our struggles too, first against the British, which led us to undertake the Great Trek in 1837, and then against Vincent's Zulus in Natal in the mid- and late-1800s.'

Prince Vincent Zulu nodded in agreement. 'And of course there was the Boer War' added Johan, 'when my grandmother spent some of her prime years in British concentration camps. My father was in the Afrikaner struggle and was arrested by the English for having rifles and being a member of the Ossewa Brandwag.[3] Yes, we Afrikaners had our struggles too, make no mistake.

'I joined politics because, without compromising the survival of the Afrikaner, I wanted to make my contribution to breaking with the past and creating a new South Africa so that my children would want to stay rather than leave. If they do stay, we'll know we have succeeded.'

De Jager

'I can identify with that,' chipped in Chris de Jager, bringing himself on stage as Johan concluded.

Said the Deputy Leader of the Afrikaner Volksunie: 'My family history goes way back too. My ancestors were in the early Cape also and left with Piet Retief in 1838. They too had trouble with Vincent's Zulus, as you remember!'

Vincent smiled shyly: 'Anyone would think by the way you people talk that I am the father and personal owner of the Zulu nation. A slight exaggeration, I think!'

'Well, our bigger problems, Vincent, were with the British who were always "the enemy" and English was always the language of the enemy. You see, both my grandfather and my father, only fourteen at the time, went to fight in the Anglo-Boer War at the turn of the century. Their house was burned down by the British and my father's three sisters were taken to concentration camps. And for ever after we resisted efforts to force English on Afrikaners.'

(I reflected with inner amusement about my own child-hood mythology which had nearly always presented the English as the knights in shining armour galloping over the hillside to conquer and civilise the savages and get those blasted Afrikaners to stop obstructing the process and learn a decent language. Though I must admit now that my mother's parents had always said the Anglo-Boer War was a dreadful and wicked British mistake. No, we weren't lily-white after all.)

Chris went on, however, to relate one incident from their family history which was always there to temper their bitterness and to humanise the English.

'My grandfather was at the battle of Majuba in 1881 in the first Anglo-Boer War. This had begun after the British Secretary of State for the Colonies had told Theophilus Shepstone, Secretary for Native Affairs in Natal, to annex the Transvaal. In April 1877 the Union Jack was hoisted in Pretoria to huge Afrikaner protest, to make the Transvaal British. This triggered what we call our First War of Independence in 1879.

'Well,' said Chris, warming to his tale, 'the battle of Majuba near the end of this war was a disaster for the British. They lost nearly half their force of more than five hundred men. My grandfather was there and he came upon a British soldier bleeding to death on the mountain. He had a great gaping wound in his side and clearly had only moments to live. As my grandfather, rifle in hand, stood over him and offered him water, the soldier reached slowly and agonisingly into his pocket with one hand to pull out an engraved silver watch, whose lid clicked open as he pressed the catch. With his other hand he reached into the massive bleeding wound and then, smearing the blood into the underside of the watch's lid, closed it and handed it as a parting gift to my grandfather – a gift sealed in blood and signifying the madness of war. Then he died.'

There was silence. A Kolobe shrike chirped in the tree above us. We heard the sound of water trickling into the pool beside us.

'My grandfather never forgot that. He told us war and fighting were futile. There had to be another way. I believe that to this day. And I still have that watch as one of my most treasured possessions to remind me of that truth.'

But Chris wasn't through just yet. 'So now I say to you that although I am an Afrikaner and I love my people, I am not a racist. But I want to be an Afrikaner, even as I want all to be free. It's true that in despair I once joined the AWB but I only stayed six months. Then I tried the Conservative Party and Treurnicht. But their line made no space for dialogue and negotiation and everything was based on colour differentiation. So I left them and carried on with my work as an advocate. Finally I went into politics. I stood in the Bethal constituency and won. At last the Afrikaner Volksunie appeared under Andries Beyers. They stood for dialogue and non-racialism but also for an Afrikaner homeland in a federal structure. Rather like being in a big house with others, but having one room of your very own. Do you think it is bad that some of us should want that?'

There was another silence. We were all growing a bit. Then animated discussion.

The Prince and the IFP

Figuring enough allusions had been made to Vincent and his Zulus, the gentle Prince from Ulundi now spoke. He told of his childhood in the Zulu royal family, his science degree in botany and his deep feelings about the political situation.

'In my early years, political trials were constantly going on and people like Albert Luthuli were heroes to me. I identified with them and also greatly admired Mangosuthu Buthelezi, with whom I grew up. I saw the problems he had agonising over the decision of whether to work from outside the system or from within, as a thorn in its flesh. He decided on the latter and I believe he prevented many National Party projects from materialising.

'You see we were looking at the problem with the same loathing for apartheid as ANC people but with different views as to how to reach the solution we all wanted.'

The Prince then went on to affirm that it had been very painful to have the integrity and genuineness of their struggle called in question.

'For example, when I was in America for four years doing my MA and PhD, some young ANC people surrounded me one day and danced and toyi-toyed [high-stepping dance] round me in a circle shouting: "Traitor, stooge, sell-out, Gatsha's spy! You are opposing the struggle!" This was very, very painful to me because so many ANC people were my heroes. I was terribly disappointed and hurt. The fact was that my birth in the extended Zulu royal household, my life in the Ulundi area, my beliefs, and my friendship with Buthelezi had all cast me by the accidents of history to work out my destiny in the IFP. That is who I was and am. It could not be otherwise. But to be called a stooge, traitor, spy and sell-out was very bad and I was very wounded.'

I cast my eye over at Lekau, Lesaoana and John Nkadimeng. Some of Vincent's pain, even in recalling this, was now etched on their faces too.

Said Lekau: 'It is very important that we hear such things. Otherwise we fail to understand and accept each other. I think, brother Vincent, I would like to come and visit you where you are in Ulundi.'

The Zulu Prince finished his story: 'On my return to South Africa I was appointed in 1991 to be Deputy Minister of Education for the KwaZulu government. But I continued to be saddened by the ongoing IFP-ANC differences which finally led to so much violence. Perhaps there were or are fears in us about being run or governed by the other. We must get over these. We all celebrated when Mandela was released and we believed he would come and sort out the violence. And our hearts were sad when things did not take place and develop as we anticipated. But it will come right.'

It had been, I felt, a very important utterance. Scales had fallen from many eyes. And wasn't there something in North American Indian folklore which says, 'Never judge a man until you have walked five miles in his moccasins'?

Other Stories

Other stories followed. John Nkadimeng elaborated on his experiences over years and years of anguished participation in the struggle from within the SACP and ANC and his years of being shunted from one prison to another midst nightmarish privations, including being hit with knobkerries, beaten with whips and suffering chilling cold without adequate blankets in his cell.

Finally his health was so shattered at one point that his wife didn't recognise him when she came to visit him in Kroonstad Prison.

Lekau of AZAPO told how being a victim of forced removals and seeing so many people die turned him to politics: 'The experience of black people under apartheid is what politicised me. And I made Steve Biko my hero because he taught us black consciousness and urged us to celebrate our blackness and fight till we had won true and full liberation.'

Rupert Lorimer, with fun and humour, described his 'chequered career', as he put it, going to Wits University with South African Communist Party Leader Joe Slovo and then dropping out to get into African theatres as a backroom boy till finally he was senior stage director.

'I was even offered a singing position in an Italian opera and nearly took it! Then in London I worked as a dishwasher in a restaurant while looking for theatre work. At last back in South Africa I went into the building industry, started my own business and then went into politics. In fact when I stood for the Progressive Party in the hopeless, lost-cause seat of Orange Grove in a fit of absentmindedness, and then won, I felt I had almost got into Parliament by accident!

'Our struggle was the battle to try and convince whites. Vincent and the IFP were doing their bit from another vantage point and with another group. And Buthelezi did very important work for years at the forefront of the internal struggle, especially against P.W. Botha. The point is that the struggle had so many different dimensions and it is a shame when people are intolerant of any dimension but their own.'

And so new friendships were born with every syllable of every story as each unfolded.

Added Lekau: 'I learned more in my first three hours at Kolobe than I could have done in six years anywhere else.'

NEW SOUTH AFRICA

In the final hours of Sunday as we looked to the future and discussed our visions of the new South Africa and how to get there, it was with hearts burning with common purpose, despite different strategies. The company of strangers had become the fellowship of friends.

George Wanjau closed the time with prayer and then added: 'Why don't we link hands and say the Lord's Prayer.' That's bold, I thought.

'Our Father, which art in heaven . . .' I opened my eyes to peep.

SACP Central Committee member John Nkadimeng, his eyes closed and looking heavenward, was gripping the hands of AVU's Chris de Jager and PAC's Lesaoana Makhanda.

'. . . Hallowed be Thy Name . . . Thy Kingdom come . . .' I closed my eyes.

'. . . Forgive us our trespasses . . .'

Kolobe One had come to an end.

5 Lessons for Life

All life is meeting.

Martin Buber

It is all a question of communication and coming to understand one another and seeing one another as real people. Then one wants to relate.

Ruth Mompati of the ANC

Kolobe One had ended, but the Kolobe process had only just begun. In all there were five more such weekends throughout 1993 for some ninety senior politicians and one for some forty-eight younger ones, the majority of the latter coming to a weekend in Natal.

That the process was working was confirmed to Peter and me the following week when AZAPO's Lekau rang from Pietersburg: 'Hello, Mike. It's Lekau. How are you, brother? I want to see you at AE sometime. And can you give me Vincent's phone number in Ulundi? I want to go see him.' Later in the year he brought no less than thirteen AZAYO (Azanian Youth Organisation) leaders to the Political Youth Leaders' weekend.

Next day John Nkadimeng rang Peter: 'My friend, would you send me some books on Christianity? By the way, that was one of the best weekends I ever had!'

We had little doubt that the December 1992 experience cried out for as much and as extensive repetition as we could manage in the following year prior to the elections.

Maybe the Kolobe spirit could spread – like leaven in a lump. South Africa could do with it for sure.

So we proceeded. And the Kolobe kaleidoscope became to our hearts and minds one of the most instructive experiences any of us had ever gone through.

Lessons seemed to abound and proliferate – most of them simple and almost self-evident – yet easily missed and in some ways seldom heeded.

What were they – these lessons for life – and for a lifetime? And for the future? Even the long-term future? Or even for other parts of the world where gaps between people or groups of people are commonplace?

I God is there

The Kolobe experience operated, for those of us behind it, on theistic presuppositions that God is there, that He is alive and real, all-powerful and all-loving, and is the Creator of the world and all in it.

In other words we brought to the exercise a theistic world view in which the natural and supernatural, nature and supernature meet, connect and intermingle – whether we realise it or not.

As we noted in the preface, our world view is important, because it affects our approach to everything as well as our interpretation of what happens around us.

II Prayer pays off

Not only did we pray before, during and after each Kolobe weekend, but we asked many other prayer friends to do likewise. In fact this was a key to the beautiful atmosphere which prevailed against all odds. In none of the six Kolobe weekends did we ever have any hostility or heat enter the situation at all. This was remarkable.

And if anyone thinks you can't pray for a bunch of

tough politicians, just remember the little girl in pyjamas who, as she left a big dinner party hosted by her parents, announced to the assembled guests: 'I'm going to say my prayers. Anyone want anything?'

Yes *anything*. We can pray about *anything*!

III Getting away is good

Getting away is a key component if dialogue is to achieve full potential and impact. To have attempted it in the city at a private home or hotel would have been hopeless. But getting right away to a place of beauty and isolation seems, in the freshness and newness of the environment, to open people up to each other, to new things and to the chemistry of change.

IV Privacy builds mutual confidence

A corollary of getting away is that privacy is possible, another critical ingredient if a dialogue exercise of this sort is to succeed. Not everyone would have wanted it known who they were with, lest supporters should interpret all this as fraternising with the enemy.

So the absence of the press and media became vital to the process. Not that they don't provide a valuable service. But in the case of Kolobe, our cause was best served by keeping it all out of media spotlight or knowledge.

Interestingly enough, at the end of Kolobe One, ten out of eleven participants were not only happy but eager to tell the world about our experience, because, as several observed: 'South Africa is so short of good news stories, and here we have one.' But one participant had reservations and was nervous. We felt his anxiety should be honoured. And that was that. This helped build mutual trust and confidence.

Being away from it all also provided security for big

shots even though some took the double precaution of bringing their bodyguards!

Rod, our on-site security expert, amused us by psyching out how many weapons a given bodyguard was carrying: 'Three,' he would whisper to me with a grin, 'one at his right hip pocket, one under his left shoulder, and one under his trouser leg, along his right calf.' I obliged by looking suitably impressed.

On one Kolobe visit, when my wife Carol and I were sharing two halves of a bungalow with Benny Alexander and his bodyguard, we tiptoed in late to find Benny and friend already asleep, the latter in the lounge outside Benny's room through which Carol and I had to pass. Our desire not to disturb the weary knew no bounds that night as we tiptoed like mice to our room with lively imaginations visualising the bodyguard waking to a footstep in the dark and, with hair-trigger reaction, seizing his weapon and firing into the dark. At which end of Kolobe, life and fellowship with Benny and Co. for one well-meaning evangelist plus spouse!

In fact one night when Benny and bodyguard were out, and I was en route to an early bed, I thought for fun to check under the latter's pillow. Sure enough a sizeable and lethal weapon lay beneath his pyjamas! My sense of mischief tempted me greatly to remove it and perhaps leave a chocolate or Bible verse as a healthier bed-time companion, but discretion became the better part of valour, and I refrained!

But, yes, the interests of trust, mutual confidence, confidentiality and freedom of conversation were served by being away from it all in a place of privacy and security.

V Fun is freeing

Another conclusion is that most of us, whether in church, state, business, or whatever, rush to agendas in our various endeavours or committee meetings before real relationships, trust or understanding are in place. Achieving the agenda items consequently becomes tortuous, problematic and sometimes impossible. The importance of finding one another in our common humanity before we rush to agenda or complex debate is, I believe, a crucial principle for progress, especially in situations of dramatic human diversity or complexity.

The extraordinarily simple, self-evident, yet often ignored expedient of just having plain fun together is a key component of what Rupert Lorimer called 'the winning formula of Kolobe'.

How could the PAC's Benny Alexander and Addie van Rensburg, an associate of right-wing leader General Constand Viljoen, feel the same about one another once they'd clambered up a hillside together to look at Bushman paintings, or 'oohed and aahed' at the baby rhino in the breeding pen or walked into the bush together, to everyone's amusement, to answer a call of nature?

'Who's going to kill whom behind that bush?' called out Lampie Fick, National Party MP and Deputy Minister of Home Affairs, as the two opposing heavies vanished from view.

As they returned, Benny, by now in a hilarious mood, announced: 'We've just solved all South Africa's problems. Addie and the General are all joining the PAC and the PAC is going to give the Afrikaners a volkstaat!'

Other pictures of fun – mental snapshots as it were – come to mind. A trio of political foes toasting 'the new South Africa' while clustered under a shared waterproof cape as rain threatened during a bush picnic. A non-swimmer SACP heavy stepping gingerly but joyously into the pool togged up and squeezed into my spare pair of overly tight khaki shorts. And Danie Schutte, Minister of Home Affairs, watching on TV the rugby test of the Springboks versus the French surrounded by liberation movement blacks and political opponents of all shades and stripes, all enjoying the cut and thrust of constant banter as they supported the French against Danie the Springbok!

I often thought during these fun times that they would have provided the ideal context in which people like Andries Treurnicht or Eugene Terreblanche could have made revolutionary discoveries of their fellow South Africans. But Treurnicht refused point blank to come or let his CP leadership attend, interested though some were, while Terreblanche, after some initial openness, banged down his phone on me along with some rude words, when he heard ANC were participating in the weekends. That made me very sad.

But shared fun is not enough to break from superficial to genuine friendship and understanding. That requires grasping in depth why the other person is as they are and why they act or believe as they do.

VI We are all products of our histories

It was again and again extraordinary as autobiographies were shared to grasp the degree to which each of us had been shaped, whether positively or negatively, by the accidents of history and the course of our personal lives.

One person shaped positively by extraordinary hardship and suffering over half a lifetime was Elizabeth Sibeko, the present Project and Development Secretary for the PAC. But what a story!

With the log fire burning in the boma, the faces of all flickering in and out of light and shadow, and attention absolutely rapt, Elizabeth told us her tale of struggle, tragedy, trial and finally triumph as her spirit rose to overcome and forgive the past.

Like all blacks, she and her husband David deplored and hated apartheid and what it inflicted by way of the destruction of human dignity and self-esteem. Hence their deep involvement in the struggle which led to David's arrest while trying to flee the country. He was brought back by the police who then searched the house. 'I had two little children who were terrified when they saw their father with handcuffs, and the police, black and white, in the house,' confessed Elizabeth.

David's situation did not look hopeful because, among his colleagues, they had discovered bombs. He was refused bail and Elizabeth, expecting her son Temba at the time, left the High Court crying and shivering. In due time David was acquitted for lack of hard evidence, but this only led to further harassment from the Security Branch. 'Day and night they came,' said Elizabeth, 'till life became so unbearable that we felt we must escape.'

In the process they were arrested thirteen times trying to get through Botswana and Zambia, and the family spent six weeks sleeping under trees and bushes. At times they were terrified by elephant, rhino or hippo as they trudged by day and were traumatised with fear by night. A lion even sniffed at them one night as they lay transfixed and paralysed with terror.

Eventually David and Elizabeth reached Tanzania and were then transferred to London in 1969 where David was appointed to represent the PAC. They were later moved to the United States to represent the PAC at the UN.

At one point David had to go back to Tanzania to attend to PAC affairs. Both he and Elizabeth sensed danger and spoke of this together. But the risk was taken. David, a journalist, had the as-yet-unpublished information on government slush funds and the Eschel Rhoodie story of fraudulent handling of government monies. When it broke, the 'Muldersgate Scandal', so-called because of its alleged linkage to cabinet minister Connie Mulder, brought down the government of Prime Minister John Vorster. Sibeko seemingly had this inside track data and suspected that government security agents were after him. So too possibly were certain dissenters within the ranks of the liberation movement.

In any event, one or other group got to him and he was assassinated in Tanzania. Said Elizabeth with emotion: 'My life was wrecked because I felt I could not go on without him.'

Four children had lost a father and Elizabeth a husband. Although she had been brought up in a Christian home, this became a turning point for Elizabeth. 'I was very disturbed by it all. I mourned dreadfully, and it was very painful. I cried and cried before the Lord asking why, why, why this manner of terrible death? I could not understand why this should happen because David had never hurt anyone and had always worked for good. I read my Bible for answers, but I still could not understand people who kill and destroy. I blamed the Devil!'

Elizabeth then told us how she turned her back on God at that point. 'When I finally saw my husband's grave, I bought a second grave for myself.

'However, God had not turned His back on me,' she added, 'because through a UN ambassador and his wife, I was brought back to Christ and the church and surrendered to Him my pain and bitterness. I was also miraculously healed of cancer which had begun to develop before David's death.'

Finally in 1990, as a result of President de Klerk's famous decision, she could return to South Africa where 'all I want to do after twenty-eight years in exile is to live out my life in reconciliation towards others and in helping build the new South Africa.'

When Elizabeth was finished, a hush descended on us. Once again, none of us knew quite how to respond.

I remember Danie Schutte, then Minister of Home Affairs, a rug pulled over his knees to protect from the late night air, staring long and hard into the fire. The fact was that to know such a story was to be given an explanation for the sense of courage, graciousness and determination etched into the face, features and faith of Elizabeth Sibeko.

She was a product of her history. And a good one. And good or bad, we are all products of our histories. That's why knowing one another's histories makes each of us more explicable to the other.

'I don't think I've ever told my whole story like that before,' she mused. I guessed she had told only the half of it.

The fire was now dying and whispering that the day was over. We prayed and turned in.

VII To know all is to forgive all

A story illustrating this principle comes coincidentally from another senior PAC official, this time from Johnson Philip Mlambo, Deputy President and former Commander-in-Chief of APLA.

I had always thought 'one settler, one bullet' was such a dreadful slogan, but what makes a person embrace such a slogan?

Johnson's story and history helped me understand and forgive without condoning. Had I walked his path or shared his suffering, might I too have been thus radicalised?

As with so many others, Johnson spent a large portion of his life on Robben Island, having been charged with conspiracy to commit sabotage. He arrived on 26 June 1963. 'The whole place was sandy and pushing a fully loaded wheelbarrow was very hard. On the very first day there I had a runny tummy. It was such that when I got a break to relieve myself, I found that terrible blisters had developed which burst and became open, bleeding wounds. I was one among many who experienced that and we were advising each other to apply our own urine to this. When you are working with continuous assaults on you and you get open wounds, this was the only remedy we had.

'On one occasion, we were digging trenches and I was

forced into one of these and covered up until only my head was above the soil. I was then urinated on by one of the warders. Sometimes, when manual work had generated great thirst, I asked for water, but was offered urine.'

A few Kolobe whites surely reflected, as I did when hearing this, 'If that had happened to me, might I just not think about "one settler, one bullet"?' As I said just now, one does not condone, but one had to understand. And one had to forgive.

Johnson pressed on with his tale: 'The type of work we did on Robben Island was such that one could not compare it with normal work. You would build a mound of soil and in two weeks you were told to take it again and dump it in another spot. It was punishment. It was not serving a purpose.

'But I discovered that human beings are very strong. I experienced being hit on the back of the head and collapsing. After I was knocked down, they would follow with beatings on my back. Yet I could wake up and continue with the work.

'One of the most humiliating things was to find that the prison guards actually connived with the common-law prisoners to prepare nice food to entice some of the young people who were starving to be involved in homosexual practices. At one stage our PAC prisoners took the position that we would not allow these things to continue.'

It was in this effort that Johnson lost his right eye. 'We had decided to take only our normal food rations. We resolved that no one in our midst would receive special food. But someone did take special food and, as we dumped the food in the toilets, while we were still struggling to get the dish away from him, he thrust his thumb into my eye socket. That is how I lost my eye.'

Johnson told how sometimes people died right in front of them. Others became desperately ill. 'We had one fellow prisoner who was serving a fifteen-year term. When he had only eighteen months to go, he died from cancer which had been ignored for a long time. He would complain, but the prison doctor would dismiss him and tell him he was acting up. Ultimately he was taken to a hospital on the mainland through the intervention of a doctor from the international committee of the Red Cross. But unfortunately it was too late to save him.'

He also told how he was one of the first people on Robben Island to further his studies. 'In 1967 I passed the first part of my BSc Economics though London University. But when I was to do the last part, I was found with some newspapers, which was a big crime. I had to spend six months in isolation for that and was not allowed to study for years. That privilege was only restored in 1975 and in 1977 I was finally able to complete the degree.'

Very painful for Johnson and others was being cut off from family and friends and from the opportunity, never to come again, of marrying and having a family. 'We were supposed to have one visit and one letter every six months. I had about five visits from my brother. My mother passed away in 1967 at a time when she was thinking of making a trip to see me.'

On 20 June 1983, twenty years after going to prison Johnson Mlambo was finally released on completion of his sentence.

Had half a lifetime been wasted? 'No,' said Johnson, 'you must understand we did not see this as wasted effort. For we were fighting to have our worth realised and recognised and to resist the notion that if one was black, one was insignificant, regardless of what you had achieved.'

And so to the Deputy Presidency of the PAC.

One might not condone all, but the more one knows the more one can forgive.

VIII To hear the other side is to see one's own culpability

The Kolobe encounters, and the process of listening to one another's stories, had the astonishing effect of causing people to lift blame and judgment on others and acknowledge varying degrees of their own guilt and culpability for inflicting pain, rejection, oppression or misunderstanding on others.

In South Africa, scapegoating and laying blame at all doors but one's own are habits we have developed into an art form. And many other situations of conflict around the world reveal the same peril. So what's new since the Garden of Eden when Adam blamed the woman and the woman blamed the serpent?

But we saw again and again at Kolobe as people shared their stories and perhaps their pain, others came to see where they had contributed to that pain. As the old English proverb says, 'a guilty conscience needs no accuser'. And in such moments, when consciences are pricked without accusers, repentance can be born, confession be made and forgiveness be granted. That way the spiral of blame and counter-blame is broken and new situations are created.

IX Full understanding opens the door to real relationships

To forgive all, confess all and understand all also opens the door to real relationships which cannot otherwise be born. Understanding shatters stereotypes and explodes false mythologies about the other person.

For example, Lampie Fick, a cabinet minister in the South African government, felt himself bristling within when Jacob Dikobo, boss of AZAPO's Northern Transvaal Education Secretariat, began in one of the Kolobes to tell his tale. Later he confessed: 'What hit me between the eyes this weekend was that although I had grown up to hate AZAPO and people like Jacob, now I can feel and empathise with him because I have learned from him about his experiences. How can I hate someone I now know as a real flesh and blood human being?'

Said Carel Boshoff, Jr, H.F. Verwoerd's grandson and strong propagator of an Afrikaner volkstaat out of Kolobe, 'I understand in new ways why blacks want what they do, and I think they understand me and my cries a bit better as well. And we can relate.'

One lovely person from a few of the younger leaders who came to Kolobe was Vimleka Rajbansi, daughter of the veteran Indian politician, Armichand Rajbansi. When she came to share her story she said: 'If I were telling this story only twenty-four hours ago, it would have been radically different. But last night I sat up late talking and listening to several conservative Afrikaners. Their stories have profoundly affected me and changed my attitudes to Afrikaners completely. All in the space of one day!'

Aubrey

I personally was particularly impacted by exposure to communists, a group which had been totally demonised by my background conditioning and by the previous South African governments. Not that I could ever have any brief for communism, which I believe to be in error philosophically, theologically, ideologically and economically. But prior to Kolobe One, I had not really known any communists as human beings. John Nkadimeng first opened up my heart to the humanity of communists. Others followed. Then came Aubrey Lekwane of the SACP, a young man of immense gifts, buoyant disposition and radiant smile.

I remember being deeply moved as he shared of his search for God, which was in process when he was arrested and put in prison.

'In Pretoria Central Prison I called on God to rescue me and come to me, but He seemed to abandon me. So I turned away from Him and became a communist.'

'But Aubrey,' I interjected, 'you were in prison only six months. I think He did rescue you.'

Other prison experiences of Aubrey Lekwane impacted us all, as when he later went to visit a friend in Pretoria Central Prison. As he was being guided to the meeting place, he suddenly saw another friend of long ago, his face ashen and stricken, being led along the corridor between two warders.

The man's face exploded with joy when he saw Aubrey.

'Oh Aubrey, Aubrey, I knew you'd come. You have a stay of execution for me. You do, don't you? Surely you do. You do, you do, don't you? Tell me.' His agonised and anguished eyes were pleading.

It was Aubrey's turn to go ashen and stricken as he realised in stark horror that his friend was at that very moment being led to the gallows.

'And I had to tell him,' continued Aubrey in visible distress as he recollected the episode, 'that I did not know of his situation and I had no stay of execution. I had in fact come to see someone else. My friend's face suddenly stiffened and with head held high and eyes cold, resolute and set straight ahead, he walked past me, without even a sideways glance at me and continued on his lonely walk to death.'

Modest measures of understanding began to seep into our souls. And it worked the other way round for Aubrey himself as he too listened to others.

'When I leave here,' he said, 'and find I know only someone's name or political position, it is going to be so totally inadequate. I realise now what I have missed in not knowing more about others.'

'Yes,' observed the ANC's Ruth Mompati, whose own full story she said she had never told before, 'it is all a question of communication and coming to understand one another and seeing one another as real people. Then one wants to relate.'

At the end of that particular Kolobe, I saw National Party MP Derck Christophers getting Ruth Mompati's address and phone number from her.

'It's just so that I know who to ring up when I want to give the ANC hell!'

Both laughed. Yes, real relationships are birthed on the wings of full understanding.

X Finding one's neighbour is both revolutionary and costly

For Andries Beyers, leader of the Afrikaner Volksunie, and one-time senior colleague of Andries Treurnicht in the Conservative Party, the experience at Kolobe had enormous implications. In fact it contributed to his eventual renunciation of the volkstaat policy which in the end led to his resignation as both leader and member of his party.

'You see, that weekend, which admittedly I went to under pressure, was the very first time in my life I had communicated with black leaders on a personal level. And I found what I had missed all these years in terms of real communication with my fellow South Africans. In fact I came to realise I simply did not know my fellow South Africans.

'The only personal contact I had had with blacks previously was as an employer and them as my workers. And my vision of revolutionary black leaders was to see them as my future oppressors. That was the reason for my now-abandoned belief in a volkstaat policy. But at Kolobe I said to myself, "These people are not so bad after all and it won't be disastrous living with them as compatriots and fellow citizens. In fact this Kolobe experience tells me we can even work together."

'There was something else,' added Andries. 'It related to where God fitted in. First of all, I felt we Afrikaners had, to a certain extent, a monopoly on God and that He would always be on our side. Second, to be on God's side meant being against the ANC because they were atheists and on the side of the Devil. But at Kolobe I saw there were also Christians in the ANC and in other black liberation movements. This was revolutionary to me.'

So, as Andries later reported: 'I now had to work on the implications of this. It contributed to my newly developing conviction that our answers lay in a non-racial South Africa, though federally constituted.'

He later resigned as leader and member of the AVU, admittedly not to join the ANC, but to join the then-President de Klerk's National Party.

'Yes,' Andries said to me one day on the phone, 'I sit now as an MP in our new non-racial Parliament and effectively as part of a new non-racial government. And I am hopeful for the future. And, to a certain extent, it all began at Kolobe.'

Addie van Rensburg
Something similar happened to Addie van Rensburg, one-time associate of the late Andries Treurnicht and of General Constand Viljoen, and a member of the National Executive of the Afrikaner Volksunie. Addie came to four Kolobes. A convert indeed. And each time bringing someone else from the right wing to whose leaders after each weekend he preached and preached the message, experience and importance of dialogue and negotiation.

Nor was his own story uninteresting. Born and raised and conditioned in the north west town of Brits, best known for its extreme right-wing sentiments, Addie was well set to become a big-time right-winger himself.

His great-grandfather had been a president of the 'Zuid-Afrikaanse Republiek'. His mother came from the Strijdom family which produced a former prime minister of South Africa.

It was during the period of negotiations that Andries

Beyers, then leader of the Afrikaner Volksunie, asked him to attend a dialogue weekend on behalf of the AVU. 'I could not have asked for a worse start to my venture into big-time right-wing politics than spending a weekend of dialogue and socialising with the "enemy".'

But at Kolobe his attitude began to change radically: 'Facing people who were on the wrong side of the apartheid fence made me realise with shame and sadness that apartheid had become a monster which dehumanised people and subjected them to the most degrading laws and regulations, and all in an attempt to preserve a *status quo* which could no longer be defended. The stories shared by people such as Elizabeth Sibeko and Philip Mlambo, to mention only two, had a devastating impact on me and on the hearts and minds of everybody present.

'In fact, Kolobe proved to me that the biggest problem we face in South Africa is one of perceptions. We talk about each other rather than to each other. And we form perceptions of each other based on hearsay. Then through those false perceptions, we fan the flames of hatred which are threatening to devour our country.'

As Addie got back to Brits after each successive weekend, things seemed to get hotter and hotter for him as the human revolution in his heart took place. 'You see, to the Afrikaners of Brits, my associating with communists and terrorists and speaking in praise of people like Mandela and Ramaphosa was the ultimate act of treason. One particularly nasty and humiliating incident made my wife, who accompanied me on one of the weekends, remark, "Maybe we should never have gone to Kolobe, for then we would still be able to live in peace with our friends."'

But there was no going back. For they had opened themselves up to something greater than fear and hatred. 'So while I love my own people deeply and will always be an Afrikaner, I will never again be part of a system which denies other people the opportunities I have had. I found at Kolobe that the love of our Lord Jesus Christ lives in the hearts of many people, and in reaching out to our fellow people there are many willing hands to grasp one in reconciliation.'

Addie, like Andries Beyer, also resigned from his political party and embarked on what he called 'the greater work of trying to bring people together. Especially did I work hard on seeking to persuade Constand Viljoen (then leader of COSAG, the Concerned South Africans' Group) and others to enter negotiations fully and contest the election.'

Later Danie Schutte stated: 'I believe Kolobe had a significant part in finally getting the right wing into the elections.' And people like Addie had really done their bit in this regard.

With South Africa's wide variety of race groups and cultures, many people have little knowledge or understanding of people they have never been exposed to. 'A large majority of Afrikaners live in the Transvaal and Orange Free State,' Addie stated, 'and have no experience in relating to coloured people. The time that I was able to spend getting to know Clifford Nasson of the DP was so important to me as an Afrikaner and is something I will never forget.'

Addie also on one occasion in Pietersburg sought out AZAPO General Secretary Don Nkadimeng, brother of John, whom he'd met on one of the weekends. 'We had just found each other as human beings, though we were "the political impossibles". We had an amazing time!'

Yes, Andries and Addie found their neighbours and it was both revolutionary and costly in terms of very significant practical implications for their lives.

XI Right relationships enable the pursuit of sound agendas.

The Kolobe weekends and the relationships they produced constantly illustrated the above principle. Agendas of complexity or difficulty or requiring seemingly impossible partnerships can be pursued once trust, understanding and relationships are in place.

Not only did Addie and others demonstrate this as they worked to open up the right wing, but even practical projects took new life and meaning, as when the NP's Derek Christophers and the DP's William Mnisi found themselves post-Kolobe combining forces in a Peace Accord project in a Reef township.

Likewise my colleague, Peter Kenton-Johnson and I were able to combine with Hassen Ebrahim, Co-ordinator of the ANC's Negotiating Commission at the World Trade Centre, and with Beryl Baker, Dr Mandela's personal assistant, both of whom came to Kolobe, to try and get 'the Big Three' (Mandela, de Klerk and Buthelezi) together for a Kolobe weekend, or, failing that, 'the Big Eight' – the heads of all the major parties. That we did not succeed was due more to the impossibilities of synchronising diaries at the end of 1993 than to failures of teamwork among new-found friends.

Then there were some bold combined endeavours from the final Kolobe weekend in November 1993, on the one hand to get COSAG to jump on to the electoral train before it got too far away, and on the other to persuade the government and the ANC to stop the train and reverse back into the station to collect the stragglers. In this exercise Inkatha National Chairman, Frank Mdlalose (now Premier of KwaZulu-Natal), and National Party MP Johan Marais, both of whom had been at the last Kolobe, worked together with others of us to attempt what seemed and in fact proved impossible at that time.

But the point is, the endeavour was earnestly made and as Johan Marais later noted, such things were possible because at Kolobe 'issues came into proper perspective as we got to know others and their perspectives on life and shared with those we would otherwise have seen as opponents but who had now become friends, even if we still had different political views.'

For us in AE, one Kolobe serendipity was the formal request from PAC leadership to facilitate communication between the political and armed wings of the movement in winding down the armed struggle and the terminating of the 'one settler, one bullet' slogan. We co-operated in this endeavour during the last weeks of 1993 and the early weeks of 1994.

Most significant of all was what came forth in March and April 1994 in terms of the electoral process. Our new-found depth of relationships and trust emerging from Kolobe with Home Affairs Minister Danie Schutte and IFP National Chairman Frank Mdlalose bore special fruit.

But that is a story for later chapters.

XII Ultimate identity is not to be found in the penultimates of politics

The final Kolobe lesson to many was that there is more to life than politics! And one's final identity is found not in the political but in the spiritual.

Young Andries Pienaar, AVU spokesperson at the World Trade Centre talks, though only in his early twenties and with us for the final Kolobe, seemed to be pointing us to this in terms of his own odyssey.

'I always took a keen interest in politics and the affairs of state. I did a lot of historical research on nationalism as an ideology and a lifestyle. I then became involved in writing and Afrikaner politics at the age of sixteen. I was the provincial leader in the Cape Province of the AWB Youth League. I was considered an intellectual at a very early age and, if you are young, well-spoken and ambitious, you can really climb in right-wing organisations. At twenty-one, I was admitted to Toekomsgesprek, a secret writing society, the equivalent of the Broederbond, for forwarding Afrikaner nationalism.

'But I was never at peace with myself, and the more I became involved with politics the more I struggled to reconcile my intellectual world with my world of faith, because in the Afrikaans culture, they are two separate worlds to a large extent. But then I began to see I no longer had to live in two worlds and I did not have to be inconsistent. That meant accepting every person and believing that every person was equal before God.

'Looking back on my experiences, I can see that many committed Christians are still locked into this schism of two separate worlds. Even though the Afrikaner community is so deeply rooted in the Church and the Bible, the ordinary person has not yet started taking the Bible into every part of his life. But once the Lord has led someone to grasp that necessity – and I have seen this during the election period with Afrikaners – their whole world changes and, ironically, they feel a lot more secure. They begin to realise that there is more to life than politics and power.'

Andries went on to note that Afrikaners now have to find their primary identity in terms of their faith and the Kingdom of God. 'You see, the whole world of many Afrikaner people is falling apart and, if you don't have spiritual security and a world view that makes sense, you are in trouble.

'This is a lesson of life for all, not just Afrikaners.'

Likewise all those other lessons of life from that strange and colourful corner of our country called Kolobe.

6 Pulling Together

It was church and business that often saved the day.
                                        Bishop Stanley Mogoba

While some of us were involved through 1993 on activities
such as Kolobe, lots of other little Davids were doing lots
of other things, much of it spiritually motivated, and all
of which contributed significantly to the final political
breakthrough and the downfall of the apartheid Goliath.

In fact South Africa, albeit paradoxically considering
its racial sins, is one of those places in the world where
huge numbers of people do in fact have a strong God-
awareness in their lives, activating much that they do, and
constituting the driving inspiration for the contributions
they bring.

More than that, a deep sense of urgency through these
years fuelled a spirit of pulling together with everyone,
Dunkirk-like, doing their bit. Several of these endeav-
ours and organisations bear highlighting, especially the
Institute for a Democratic Alternative for South Africa
(IDASA), the Consultative Business Movement (CBM),
the Rustenburg Churches Conference and the National
Peace Accord.

IDASA

IDASA was founded by Dr Frederick van Zyl Slabbert,
one-time leader of the opposition in Parliament, and Dr

Alex Boraine, former President of the Methodist Church and a colleague of van Zyl Slabbert's in the Progressive Federal Party, as well as an eloquent and godly voice for justice and non-racial democracy in Parliament.

In February 1986, both men dropped a bombshell on the nation by announcing that they were resigning their party positions and leaving Parliament. Eight months later they founded IDASA as a forum and force 'to help bridge the gap between the polarised worlds of parliamentary and extra-parliamentary politics in South Africa'. Central also to their concerns was the building of what they called 'a democratic culture' which was conspicuous by its absence at that time.

The endemic violence of those years led van Zyl Slabbert to comment in an IDASA publication:

Nothing exposes the bankruptcy of politicians more brutally than violence; nothing betrays the fragility of the social order easier than its consequences; nothing challenges the quality of a country's leadership as unrelentingly as its continuation. Violence makes nonsense of civility, of 'talks about talks', of negotiating democracy. There can be no democracy without a democratic culture. And any culture that depends on, or draws its inspiration from violence and brutality negates culture and democracy. The hallmark of democratic negotiation is tolerance for difference and respect for diversity. Violence is its unholy antithesis.[1]

As a counterblast to this culture of violence, hundreds of seminars and workshops were conducted all over the nation in the next eight years by a large group of predominantly young, dedicated staff around the country. Among these were Max Mamase, Eric Mntonga and Paul Graham.

Reflects Paul: 'Going into IDASA was for me a calling, something I felt God wanted me to do. It was an expression of my faith commitment. I first remember discussing my desire to make a wider contribution in South Africa with van Zyl Slabbert and Alex Boraine when they were both at the National Initiative for Reconciliation (NIR) Conference in 1985. They had just left Parliament and had gone to the NIR to meet other concerned leaders from all over to discuss their own future. At the time I was lecturing in adult education at Natal University and teaching organisational skills to angry young black activists and so-called "comrades", on the assumption that training them with these skills would help keep their contribution rational, legal and democratic. We called our project the "Comrades Marathon" after the famous road race! But at the NIR van Zyl and Alex fired me with some of their reflections and vision which eighteen months later gave birth to IDASA. I think for all of us, it was not just a job, but a calling. We wanted to make a difference.'

It was a struggle at first for IDASA with the great risk of being crushed between the suspicions of the far left and the repressive measures taken by the state on the right. As Boraine said in an interview shortly before retiring as executive director, 'The state did its damnedest to try to close us down.'[2]

He talked about the activities of IDASA as 'quiet, steady, bridge-building work which took place during the state of emergency when there were no bridges available. IDASA became a bridge and sometimes, I suppose, like all bridges, we got walked on.'[3]

It was also tense and often dangerous work, with their initial focus on negotiation politics in contrast to the politics of exclusion and repression, on the one hand, and the politics of resistance, on the other.

The danger in IDASA's work was highlighted for them when the hugely gifted Eric Mntonga was assassinated in 1987, their first year of operation, seemingly for incurring the wrath of some of Ciskei's political leadership.

'Basically,' reflected Paul, 'we believed in the fundamental goodwill of everybody in South Africa on all sides and operated on the assumption that people really did want to talk to one another, even when they denied it. I remember when right-wing involvement in the elections was really under threat, we worked to keep the generals (leaders in the right-wing movement) in the process and our staff even worked on some of the agreements between them and the ANC. We could not have done this had we not been plugging away at this kind of bridge-building work for years.'

Paul also noted that IDASA did not shy away from tackling sacred cow issues such as the role of the military, or the place of ethnicity or the concept of a volkstaat. 'I think we were a vehicle needed by God and by that moment in history.'

I am in full accord. IDASA's contribution through the terrible transition years of 1987 through to 1994 was of incalculable importance, especially in persuading grassroots opposition structures, plus rank and file white supporters of the system, to embark on the democratic alternative with both its perils and possibilities. It was cutting-edge stuff and South Africa will always be in debt to those intrepid politicians who in faith stepped out of the sacred precincts of Parliament to join others on the long march towards a democratic future.

CONSULTATIVE BUSINESS MOVEMENT

Another crucial contribution during these years came from the Consultative Business Movement, founded by businessmen such as Neal Chapman, Murray Hofmeyr, Christo Nel, and Colin Coleman. Its executive director was a longstanding friend, the Rev. Dr Theuns Eloff.

Some of us had worked in the late eighties with Theuns, as well as Caesar Molebatsi and Elias Thema of Soweto, on a project called CREID (Christian Research, Education and Information for Democracy), which in turn was birthed by the Newick Park Initiative (NPI), chaired by

Viscount Brentford of the British House of Lords. NPI was a creative and imaginative think-tank on South Africa involving a variety of concerned leaders, strategists and scholars, not only from South Africa but from the UK and Europe and a few from the USA. A key figure in NPI was Professor Washington Okumu, who later played such a critical role in the election breakthrough.

When CREID began to wind down its endeavours, Theuns' desire to make an ongoing contribution intensified, believing as he did that his faith had to have practical expression in the socio-political arena if it was to have relevance 'for such a time as this'.

'When I was approached to join the CBM which had been formed in August 1988,' Theuns said, 'it seemed the Lord was calling me to bring my contribution through this more "secular channel", as it were, rather than through the Reformed Church (Gereformeerde Kerk) of which I was a minister. In any event, after a meeting with the ANC in Dakar, Senegal in 1987, my church was not happy with my seeking to relate my faith in this way to the context around me, so I was out of favour. CBM, with its very capable and concerned board of business leaders, several of whom were committed Christians, also seeking to give practical expression to their faith, seemed to me the kind of channel I was looking for. In other words, with my way of serving the Kingdom blocked in the church, I felt I should move into society and the secular life.

'Our aim in CBM was to ensure that the business community had a role in the transformation of South Africa's political economy, as well as a non-racial democracy in a peaceful country with stability and justice. The economy was obviously being determined by the political situation, hence the phrase "political economy". It was that which we were out to impact and change.'

Although there were initially no blacks involved on the staff or board of CBM, nevertheless the body was well placed to communicate with leaders of the Mass

Democratic Movement (MDM), such as Murphy Morobe, Valli Moosa (Acting Treasurer of the UDF), and Patrick Lekhota, all of whom had been involved in dialogue with the CBM founders who had consulted with them for a long time prior to launching the CBM.

During their first year, Christo Nel, Colin Coleman, Theuns and others concentrated on enabling extensive formal contact between business leaders and the MDM via workshopping weekends where issues of every conccivable sort were thrashed out and worked through. Extensive relationships were set in place, all of which contributed finally to the ANC's unbanning in February 1990.

Then in May 1991 the government decided to call a peace conference. The ANC said publicly that they would not attend, having grave reservations about what they perceived to be a unilateral government-initiated endeavour. This left the government, the IFP and all the homeland leaders on the one hand staring across a great chasm of alienation and suspicion at the ANC, COSATU, and the Civic Movement on the other hand. At this point a confluence of concerns and initiatives came together. Moves from the church side came from Frank Chikane, General Secretary of the SACC, and Professor Louw Alberts, co-chairmen of the Rustenburg Church Leaders Committee, of which more in a moment. They made connection with CBM leadership in order to try and rescue the peace endeavour. John Hall and other business leaders from the CBM side took the initiative, along with Chikane, Alberts, Johan Heyns and Ray McCauley (all part of the Rustenburg Committee), together with the COSATU leadership, including Jai Naidoo (now Minister without Portfolio and responsible for the current Government of National Unity's Reconstruction and Development Programme). An energetic spate of shuttle diplomacy now got under way by which the government's proposed peace initiative was salvaged on the understanding that they would take no firm decisions at the first peace meeting and that later the ANC would come into the peace process with all its allies. Out of this peace exercise then came a facilitating committee of business leaders, politicians and church leaders. This effectively became the so-called Peace Committee chaired by the energetic and highly capable John Hall of Barlow Rand. Fine backstage work was also done by Archbishop Tutu, along with Chikane again and Bobby Godsell of Anglo American, to move forward the process of reaching the National Peace Accord, which will be described in a moment.

Continuing his tale, Theuns recalled that 'CBM generally, and I personally as its executive director, had to tread a very thin line between facilitating and pushing. But we tried to say to the politicians that with everyone present, they should use the momentum to get a multiparty process off the ground. But the government, for reasons of their own, decided to move more with the ANC, bilaterally, as it were. Then they would call a multiparty forum. That happened at the end of November 1991 which was the start of the CODESA (Congress for a Democratic South Africa) process. Because of our credibility and organisational back-up, by that stage we were then asked to provide the process and secretarial services for CODESA which I was asked to lead. Murphy Morobe was head of administration. There was also a CODESA secretariat which consisted of Mac Maharaj, now Minister of Transport, and Fanie van der Merwe, who was the government's Director General of Constitutional Development Services. They were to play a very important role later in the multiparty process.'

There is no doubt that business leaders, motivated by either political idealism or spiritual commitments and often both, played an indispensable role in South Africa's transition to democracy. The *Financial Mail* summed it up this way:

There has long been a relationship between the political Left and business, a relationship that is in some respects not far short of a partnership. One of the common aims has been to bring democracy to South Africa. If there had not been this relationship, the election would almost certainly not have taken place. Indeed, the business sector has come to play a part in national affairs that is surely without parallel in the world. It has oiled our transition to democracy.[4]

But make no mistake, a lot of oil was needed at times to keep the process on track, especially once Inkatha and five or six other parties, mainly on the white conservative side, pulled out of the multiparty talks in mid-1993.

World Trade Centre

The fact is that tensions intensified on all fronts with KwaZulu–Natal beginning to boil in violence and spill over ever more seriously into the Reef townships.

The right wing also became almost hysterical with war rhetoric spewing forth in ever-increasing volume, till finally on Friday, 25 June they invaded the World Trade Centre with uniformed combat 'troops' and crashed an armoured vehicle through the glass walls of the building.

I asked Theuns about his experience of that episode: 'We knew about the march of the AWB,' he replied, 'and there were numerous discussions with police, all of us saying there should not be any guns, etc. Then the police backed down to AWB threats. So they did bring their guns in. I was in the planning committee meeting, and one of the police generals was present when we heard on his radio that AWB operatives had broken through the gate. The bodyguards whisked the politicians away. I went outside and there were armed young policemen lined up against the glass wall, some trembling with fear.

Hundreds of AWB guys were running towards them with shotguns. I realised that if anybody shot there would be a bloodbath. Bullets would have gone into the crowd from inside, but also from the outside as well. But fortunately no shots were fired.

'General Constand Viljoen tried to get his people to stand back. But just then, this armoured vehicle came through the glassed wall with Eugene Terreblanche walking just behind it, having rather expeditiously climbed off the vehicle shortly before it went through the glass!

'I tried to stop the armoured vehicle by standing in front of it inside the hall. In fact, it had to stop, otherwise it would have run me over. I tried to get the people out of it, but they locked the door and I had a skirmish with some of the others. They wanted to go to the Negotiating Council where some of the delegates, especially the African delegates, were still present.

'We and the police tried to keep them down on the ground floor, but there were too many of them. They overpowered us and burst into the Negotiating Council. By that stage the others had left, and I was the only one left, and they just took over. I tried to make sure they did not break more things than they did. I was not dealing with Terreblanche directly. He came in later to the first floor, and then people from the government side came and started negotiating. I was not involved in direct negotiation.

'I was extremely angry and was very glad I did not carry a gun, which I never do, because if I had been in possession of one that day I might have used it. It was a very, very tense situation.

'After a while they dispersed. They had wanted to show the communists that they were not easily going to be taken over. They were in a strange mood combining anger with something almost festive!'

Oh well! There you go with some politics South Africa style.

In spite of all these sorts of hiccups, the negotiating process plodded on even with things becoming ever more desperate in the country, but not enough to stop the steady march of events towards the hoped-for solution.

THE ROAD TO RUSTENBURG

We mentioned the Rustenburg Church Leaders' Committee, on which I was also privileged to serve, and the part played by its Johannesburg and Pretoria members, especially Frank Chikane, Louw Alberts, Johan Heyns and Ray McCauley, in helping broker the process out of which the National Peace Accord finally came. Its story is told in *The Road to Rustenburg*, a book on the historic Conference, edited by Frank Chikane and Louw Alberts, our chairpersons. A bit of the saga is worth noting at this stage of our story.

The small town of Rustenburg in the Transvaal is better known for its export-quality oranges than its concern for a fair deal for all South Africans, irrespective of colour or creed. Ironically, it was this dusty little town in the heart of ultra-right-wing territory, which was to lend its name to the historic Rustenburg Declaration of November 1990 which unequivocally proclaims and condemns the policy of apartheid as a sin.[5]

In December 1989, 'State President Frederick Willem de Klerk appealed to the Church in South Africa to formulate a strategy conducive to negotiation, reconciliation and change.'[6]

As South Africa is such an overwhelmingly Christian nation, this 'raised few eyebrows'. Thus, because church membership represents 'about three-quarters of the total population, the Church's influence cannot be underestimated'.[7]

'On 15 June 1990, a meeting took place in . . .

Johannesburg that was to alter the course of Church history in South Africa and set the scene for the Rustenburg Declaration.'8

The gathering selected as co-chairmen Dr Louw Alberts and the Rev. Dr Frank Chikane, 'a most controversial partnership . . . between two men of God from totally opposite ends of the South African socio-political spectrum. Not since the Cottesloe Consultation in the 1960s has the Church been presented with so significant a challenge to rediscover its calling and to unite Christian witness in a changing South Africa.'9

One of the most memorable features of the conference was the spirit of confession which entered the ranks and took hold on all sides. It began with an astonishing confession from Professor Willie Jonker, a theologian from Stellenbosch University, relating to the Afrikaner's sins generally in terms of racial discrimination and apartheid, and those of the Dutch Reformed Church particularly.

'I confess before you and before the Lord,' he began, 'not only my own sin and guilt, and my personal responsibility for the political, social, economic and structural wrongs that have been done to many of you, and the results of which you and our whole country are still suffering from, but *vicariously* I dare also to do that in the name of the Dutch Reformed Church (DRC) of which I am a member, and for the Afrikaans people as a whole. I have the liberty to do just that, because the DRC at its latest synod has declared apartheid a sin and confessed its own guilt of negligence in not warning against it and distancing itself from it long ago.'10

At the end of Jonker's utterance, Archbishop Desmond Tutu, with characteristic warm-heartedness, grace and emotion, went unexpectedly and unannounced to the lectern and said: 'Our brother here has asked for forgiveness for his sins and those of his church and people, and I believe it appropriate at this time that I should on behalf of black people who suffered so much under apartheid, express that we have heard this request for forgiveness, and from our hearts we extend our forgiveness and we say that we love you and we receive you and we put the past behind us.'

Many in the conference were moved to tears and in the days that followed numbers of people from different sectors of the Church expressed similar confessions. For example, Ray McCauley confessed that the Rhema churches had for years been indifferent to socio-political issues, but that was now changing.

The fact was, as Dr Chikane and Dr Alberts said in their book,

> One man's recognition and articulation of injustice set off a chain of identification which will cause the event to go down in history as 'The Conference of Confessions', at which the church, in response to the prompting of the Holy Spirit, repented of the past and thereby set a new course for the future.[11]

Not everyone appreciated all the confessions, however, some of which were met with a measure of caution, if not scepticism. Nevertheless out of both the agony and the ecstasy of this encounter among an extremely heterogeneous group of Christian leaders, the Rustenburg Declaration came forth. For the first time in decades, possibly for the first time ever in South Africa, the Church across the board was speaking with one voice to the nation.

As would be expected, one of the issues addressed by the Rustenburg Declaration was that of violence. It concluded:

> In both Old and New Testaments God's Peace or Shalom speaks of a comprehensive wholeness and rightness in all relationships, including those between God and His people, between human and human and

between humans and creation. In South Africa, Peace and Shalom are shattered, not only by personal but also by social and structural sin. The consequences are devastating: racial alienation, mistrust, humiliation, exploitation of humans and the environment, privation of basic needs, denial of self-worth. Perhaps most devastating has been the emergence of a social climate in which violence and death rather than co-operation and life have become the norm.

One of the vital components emerging from the conference was a strategy for responding to violence, which challenged the Church to confront political and law enforcement authorities, support victims, encourage negotiation, pray for social, economic and political transformation, co-ordinate strategy through a task force and convene a peace conference to assemble leaders to help put an end to violence.[12]

The Rustenburg Conference produced a wide variety of initiatives, not least of which was the presentation of the Declaration personally by teams from the Rustenburg follow-up committee to the major political leaders and parties in the country.

NATIONAL PEACE ACCORD

One initiative taken by the members of the Rustenburg Committee in Johannesburg and Pretoria is of special note because, a year later, it brought forth the National Peace Accord.

Said Methodist Bishop Stanley Mogoba, Deputy Chairman of the National Peace Committee, 'The work of the Peace Accord was crucial in that it brought various political groups together at a time when they did not want to be together. It took a lot of time to create a rapport between members of the IFP, ANC, Communist Party, COSATU, government and all the homelands. But I think we managed to get them used to one another, so much so that in the end they were pushing the whole peace thing forward themselves.'

According to John Hall of Rand Mines and Chairman of the National Peace Committee, 'the whole process of bringing the Peace Accord into being began when President de Klerk announced a peace conference to take place in May 1991. But there was no prior consultation with the emerging political parties and the President's conference was boycotted.

'I got involved when, in attempt to make the conference all-inclusive, Jayendra Naidoo of COSATU called a meeting between business and the church, which was facilitated by Theuns Eloff and the CBM. I was invited as the chairman of the South African Chamber of Business (SACOB) to a later meeting in Khotso House with Frank Chikane, Brigalia Bam, Beyers Naude and Theuns and Jay once again. From that meeting a process of shuttle diplomacy began by our facilitating group of Archbishop Tutu, Ray McCauley, Johan Heyns, Louw Alberts and myself.

'Although church and business seemed to be strange bedfellows, it was felt that they constituted the two poles of non-political power in the country. Therefore, it made a tremendous amount of sense for them, with their collective power, to play a role in influencing the politicians. Because, first, you did not publicly defy the church very easily and, second, with business you had to keep on the ball. So together we had a powerful leverage over the politicians.'

On the involvement of the church leaders, and indeed his own as a Christian in the Peace Accord, National Peace Secretariat Chairman Dr Antonie Gildenhuys commented, 'I see it as Christian duty to do what your hands find to do wherever you are placed. My attitude is that I must do the best I can where I am placed. I believe by doing that you serve God.'

The Accord was signed in the Carlton Hotel in September 1991 midst pomp and ceremony, glitz and glitter, hope and prayer. Archbishop Tutu opened and closed the occasion with powerful prayers. And everyone was there from Mandela and Buthelezi and the Zulu King Goodwill Zwelithini through to business leaders like Bobby Godsell, who had played a major role in brokering the Accord, plus newspaper giants like Ken Owen of the *Sunday Times* and Aggrey Klaaste of the *Sowetan*.

Apart from the twenty-six political parties and trade unions, religious, financial and philanthropic organisations were also invited to sign the Accord. I warmed within when 'African Enterprise' headed the list read out! Alphabetical good fortune had smiled kindly to put us ahead of even the African National Congress![13]

In so many instances over the next two years, the Peace Accord was crucial in negotiating peaceful escapes from situations which were otherwise bound to end in violence. For example, in the wake of the massacre in Bisho, Ciskei, in 1992, John Hall recalls that 'even at the end of that ghastly day, we saw that people were uplifted because we were able to establish a way forward for the people of Ciskei and the government to reconcile.

'As some will remember, a group of people had occupied the embassy boardroom. They would not leave and the government was going to bring in the troops to clear them out. But we were able to say to those in the embassy, "You have made your point. Don't now diminish that by occupying the boardroom." So they left peacefully.

'Later in the day, the police and army were going to clear people off the road but we advised them not to do that because the people were leaving of their own accord. We tried to provide a peaceful alternative to methods that would have resulted in an escalation in hostility, the result of which would have taken that much longer to reconcile.'

Other such interventions happened in many other

places. Hall reflected on the work of the Peace Accord. 'When you're at the coalface of violence, with mobs of thousands and people shooting everywhere, firing into crowds, you can only think that this has the potential to spread countrywide and that all disputes in the future will be resolved by the heavy hand of violent force one way or the other.

'This is what it could have been. When people see the horror of violence and know what can happen, hopefully they modify their temper and anger. Talking has been so much the more powerful weapon in this country after those kinds of examples of what the violent route brought.'

In many instances where violence seemed inevitable, peaceful solutions emerged for which most people had no human explanations. As Hall said, 'Many times there were no rational explanations and I think, for the three-year period from the inception of the Peace Accord, through the elections, we saw divine intervention in the Peace Accord itself and the positive influence of the church on the process the whole time.

'I think exposure to the church in this process also had an impact on my own spiritual life. Trying to translate what I saw happening in front of my own eyes – seeing people come together and find a better way forward – I became aware of divine intervention. My favourite saying is that there are no coincidences and I think it didn't just happen. It was all a great tapestry which was being woven by God. God's hand was seen all along the line. I am not a deeply religious man but I know that it was not all my doing, that 90 per cent was with assistance from Somewhere Else.'

Though it became fashionable in the next few years to knock what the Peace Accord did not achieve, due to the environment of escalating tension, violence and civil conflict, nevertheless its efforts were gargantuan and history must surely salute it kindly.

The value of the work of those involved in the Peace Accord came home to me when Rupert Lorimer, who was in it up to his neck helping to co-ordinate scores of Reef Conflict Resolution Committees with over six hundred participants of all races, used to tell us about it at our Kolobe weekends.

'The first meetings of the Conflict Resolution Committees, which involved political and community leaders, police, churchmen and lay people, tended to be totally confrontational,' Rupert told us. 'But gradually people would realise it was pointless and sterile to accuse one another across the table. Gradually there would be an acceptance of each other's points of view, and often violence in that spot would diminish.'

He remembers one occasion when he was called to a squatter camp north of Johannesburg. 'They were having their shacks bulldozed. I rushed out there and saw the most appalling sight of shacks flattened to the ground, everything destroyed. Pets which had been tethered and chickens in cages had been flattened by the bulldozer and killed. It was horrific. People were stunned.

'Legally they should not have been there, one should admit that, but the absolute horror of destroying people's lives in that manner had nothing to do with what government was meant to be about.'

Lorimer then got hold of town councillors, the Transvaal Provincial Administration (TPA) and church leaders from the nearby towns, and took them all out to see this appalling sight of destructiveness.

He and other Peace Accord workers managed to negotiate with the army and got tents put up for shelter. For a couple of weeks people did something in the way of providing food parcels. But soon they forgot about it, and, as Rupert said in mid 1994, 'As of this moment of telling, they are still living in those tents today.'

This was heartbreaking, but who can deny the great worth of making such an effort?

Often Peace Accord workers found themselves in cross-fire situations where bullets were flying, as when someone would go into a township hostel and say that 'certain' hostile residents were coming to tear down the hostel. Then they would go to the other residents and tell them 'the Zulus' were coming out to kill them. So both sides, out of fear, would build up protective structures, and driving through the middle would be a 'bakkie' (a small open truck) of partisans firing shots in the air. The groups would then hammer each other with awful mayhem, often with Peace Accord workers trapped in it all trying to bring about a ceasefire.

And there were other kinds of intimidation as when Rupert's children were phoned anonymously with the caller saying: 'We are going to kill your father.'

Tough Times

Yes, these were tough times for all who dared to tackle the apartheid Goliath and labour for peace and democracy and a way through. Of course, the main assault on that great giant came from the surging weight and the insistent voice of the masses of ordinary men and women and especially black young people at grassroots who had said 'Enough is enough. We won't continue with this system another day if we can help it. We want freedom, dignity, equality and justice. And we want it now.'

Many of these were in mass political movements. But many were also in the churches, grannies and grandads, young men and women, mums and dads, workers and managers, all manning the ordinary machinery of daily life at a thousand levels. And of course while these were the lion, it was often left to their church leaders to make the roar.

But mostly it all began in a great surging cry of prayer from the bowels of the whole nation.

And so to that bit of the story we now turn.

7 If My People . . .

More things are wrought by prayer than this world
dreams of.

Alfred Lord Tennyson

This miracle is the product not only of our prayers and
groaning, but also of very hard work by many different
people.

Anita Kromberg of Diakonia, Durban

Throughout South Africa in the years 1991 to 1994 prayer
intensified. A great cry to God seemed to be coming from
the nation that He should act and intervene to help us,
for we could not deliver ourselves. Special prayer meetings
were constantly held in hundreds of churches. The state
and its leaders were earnestly prayed for in almost every
service of almost every church and individual people
from little old ladies, schoolboys and students through to
businessmen, housewives and factory workers were daily
calling on God for His power to be made manifest in the
national crisis. One visitor to South Africa told friends back
in the States: 'South Africa is becoming one huge prayer
meeting.'

My own conviction is that first and foremost in South
Africa's deliverance was the foundation of prayer. Many of
us through these times sought to remind people that many
things can be done after you have prayed. But nothing
really lasting will be achieved *until* you have prayed.

The depth of this prayer commitment became specially evident to some of us when we made a call in April 1993 for a prayer chain to begin operating twenty-four hours a day, round the clock, day and night, for two years.

The response was simply staggering. Hundreds and hundreds of people phoned or wrote in to say they wanted to be part of this. In the end some four thousand people became and remain part of this ongoing round the clock chain with 18 groups praying daily, 90 groups praying weekly, 108 praying monthly. This chain continues, as of now.

It even included a group of forty long-term prisoners in Fort Napier Prison in Pietermaritzburg who had found Christ in prison and who committed themselves to pray for South Africa every evening for an hour.

In Bloemfontein, the Rev. Willie Norris of Bergendal Township told of mass prayer meetings every Sunday morning at 5 a.m. This also led into a prayer chain and finally a rally in the city square in the centre of Bloemfontein where, as he put it, 'people came from all the areas, white, coloured and black. We sang, praised the Lord and prayed.'

Nearer the time of the election, another mass prayer meeting in central Bloemfontein was called. Said Willie: 'We had a very good meeting where we prayed for peace. We also had a demonstration of reconciliation with whites asking blacks and coloureds for forgiveness. All our leaders then stood in the stadium to make public statements. The meeting was very well attended, with about five thousand people there.' Norris went on: 'We are still having Friday morning prayer meetings at 6 a.m. and we usually meet at lunchtime on Wednesdays as well. The first Saturday of the month Christians meet and gather on Naval Hill and pray over the city.'

In the town Dundee in Northern Natal, Mrs Hannah Britz helped organise fourteen churches, ranging from the Dutch Reformed to the Full Gospel, to pray round the clock for the first week of every month and going on for at least a year. The fourteen churches each take one day or night to organise their own rota system to cover their given time slot.

Many elderly folk wrote in and said: 'We can't sleep well at night, so give us the 2 a.m., 3 a.m. and 4 a.m. slots!'

As the April election approached, Dean John Forbes at the Anglican Cathedral in Pietermaritzburg called for a day and night vigil running round the clock unbroken for the fifty days from Easter to Pentecost. Even local politicians were informed and invited to join in. A set of reflections and guidelines was drawn up by Derryn Hurry itemising prayer needs and political issues needing the Lord's help for resolution and listing key political figures, both provincial and national, who needed God's wisdom and power.

During one night, 153 people participated. At times, there were only one or two. Frankie Thacker, a cathedral member, reported: 'The atmosphere was often one of contrasts where the presence of God was felt in a very real way. Sometimes one tiptoed in, scarce wanting to breathe for the prayerful silence present. On other occasions glorious singing filled the cathedral.'

From the record book which participants could sign came these affirmations:

'The presence of the Lord is tangible, the silence powerful.'

'A quiet evening, I have been the only person here and yet I have not felt alone. The sense of freedom, peace and joy continues.'

Frankie Thacker adds: 'There were moments of revelation for some which came from Scripture or the daily activity surrounding them, even the cleaning of the cathedral during the vigil, a sign for some that the work of the Church in worship and service must continue unhindered despite social and political problems in the country. Always the centre of focus was the Cross and prayer. Said one: "When I came into the peacefulness of the cathedral (and this was at 1 a.m.) I saw a father in prayer and his son asleep on the carpet at the foot of the Cross. So my focus of intercession was for the young people and children who do not have the peace, security and protection of the child on the carpet."'

One busload of Christians came to spend the night. They recorded this testimony: 'During the dark hours the pain and horror of the last few years were very real. The loss of life, misery, poverty and despair of God's people was felt by all present. But as our vigil progressed we were lifted from despair. We clearly felt God saying that the nation which trusts in Him will be blessed. He will heal the land if the people who are called by His name will humble themselves, turn from their wicked ways, seek His face and pray.'

Indeed.

Assurances of prayer and prayer chain participation also came from groups in Australia, South America, New Zealand, the UK, Switzerland, Norway, the United States, Canada and all across Africa. A Zimbabwe friend wrote: 'We are praying for South Africa constantly.' Edmond Razafimanefa, president of the major church denomination in Madagascar, wrote: 'We here are always remembering South Africa in prayer.' A Kenyan lady reported: 'Thousands of Christians across Kenya were and are praying and fasting for South Africa.' A Californian woman told us: 'We were in fasting and prayer as your election approached.'

In the Old Testament God's words and promise are recorded for us in the familiar verse: '*If my people*, who are called by name, humble themselves and pray and seek my face and turn from their wicked ways, then I will hear from heaven and forgive their sin and will heal their land' (2 Chr. 7:14, my italics).

I believe that in South Africa God's people met those conditions in substantial measure and opened the way for

God's supernatural and miraculous moment of healing in the land as it came in April and May 1994. The same spiritual conditions of course need to prevail if the agonising process of healing is to continue on into the future. Let no one be mistaken about that.

But while this spirit of prayer was building up in the years from the late eighties onwards, a series of very special efforts at every conceivable level was coming forth from church leaders.

Church Leaders

Heading the list would be the indefatigable Archbishop Desmond Tutu whose up-front and backstage efforts for peace and reconciliation won him the Nobel Peace Prize in 1984. Through the decade prior to the release of Nelson Mandela, Archbishop Desmond was really the major voice, along with then Chief Minister Buthelezi, speaking from the vacuum created by the incarceration, exile or banning of so many black political leaders.

Then, in February 1990, as the gap developed between Nelson Mandela and Chief Buthelezi, the Archbishop and Methodist Bishop Mmuthlanyane 'Stanley' Mogoba were signally used of God to bring the two big leaders together on a couple of occasions.

Anglican Bishop Michael Nuttall, who with others formed the Natal Church Leaders' Group in 1988, which laid very significant foundations for inter-party dialogue in KwaZulu-Natal, recalled how the first major Mandela-Buthelezi encounter originated.

'On 15 June 1993, Desmond was here at the cathedral in Pietermaritzburg for the consecration of Peter Harker as the Bishop of Zululand. While everyone was giving the peace, Desmond went straight to Buthelezi and said, customarily, "the Peace of the Lord be with you". Then he whispered in his ear, "Would you be willing to meet with Mandela if I set something up for the two of you?"'

The psychology of the moment was masterful! And of course, with so much peace being passed around, the Chief responded positively! The deal was then clinched over tea!

Continued Bishop Michael, 'It so happened that the following day, Dr Mandela was speaking at the unveiling ceremony of the Gandhi statue, also in Pietermaritzburg. Desmond and I managed to arrange for seats on either side of him over lunch. Desmond then asked Mandela if he would be prepared to meet with Buthelezi and he agreed.'

Tutu, having brokered the whole thing on a personal level, left to go overseas leaving Nuttall and Mogoba to set it all up.

'Although it did not lead to an immediate breakthrough,' added Bishop Michael, 'our feeling is that this was part of the groundwork being laid in preparation for the final pulling together which Professor Okumu later accomplished. I believe that the higher media profile of the meeting impressed an extra sense of accountability on the two leaders. But I also feel that they were able to meet as people rather than simply as political opponents. Our concern was for "a meeting of hearts".'

Mogoba

Also involved in all this, as indicated, was Bishop Stanley Mogoba, Presiding Bishop of the Methodist Church and Deputy Chairman to John Hall on the National Peace Accord Committee.

Mogoba said that it was not easy to pull the Mandela-Buthelezi meeting off. 'You see, after making his initial contacts on a very personal level, Desmond went off to Norway and left Bishop Michael and me to make it happen! At first Mandela and Buthelezi seemed to backtrack, but I pressed them and got Desmond back for the 23 June date at the new Lutheran Centre in Kempton Park.

'It was a very fruitful encounter,' Mogoba recalled, 'which began and ended with prayer. They were initially reluctant to come together. But Desmond and I pressed them on their personal relationship, which helped because they then set aside the national agenda. By teatime we were almost there. Desmond and I ordered only two cups for them and then left the room. So they were alone together at teatimes and lunchtime, a total of about an hour and a half.'

As for the other encounters, said Mogoba, they 'were not actually joint meetings. The Chief was very angry with Mandela for certain remarks he made in his speech at the United Nations. This was a set-back for what we had tried to build up. So we had a meeting with Buthelezi again on 18 September and, two weeks later, with Mandela. By the time of the meeting with Mandela, Desmond was overseas again, so Bishop Michael and I, along with Paddy Kearney of Diakonia, sought to minister to him. We tried to discover what had gone wrong and whether we could help them get back on track.'

Mogoba paid special tribute to the Peace Accord endeavours and the work of John Hall and Antonie Gildenhuys and so many others. Of course Mogoba himself was integral in that process. 'The Peace Accord process really started with the Rustenburg Church Leaders' Conference and eventually gave birth to CODESA and the World Trade Centre exercise. After the Rustenburg Declaration had been put out we began to see new things happening. When the politicians tried to do something after that and it failed, it was church and business that often saved the day.'

As already noted (p.100) the Peace Accord was crucial in bringing various political groups together at a time when they did not want to be together. It took time to create a rapport between members of IFP, ANC, Communist Party, COSATU, government and all the homelands. But, in Mogoba's words, 'We managed to get them used to one another, so that in the end they were pushing the whole peace thing forward themselves.'

At another point Mogoba felt his efforts had been less

successful and that related to a Joint Peace-Keeping Force for which he had pleaded for two years. 'It's been a case of too little too late. Nevertheless, we are now getting all the various armies and police forces together and that's long overdue. But it's slowly working.'

In his role as leader of the Methodist Church, Mogoba said that 'Methodists were calling for a new South Africa long before it happened. We spoke about hope when there was no hope. We spoke about the new South Africa and reconciliation and negotiation long ago and at a time when people did not think we were facing reality. But slowly we began to see it happen.'

Mogoba also recalled the support the church gave to Nelson Mandela, a fellow Methodist, during his imprisonment. 'We sought to be very supportive of Mandela in prison. I actually visited him at Polsmoor with the Rev. Jack Scholtz who was President of our church. Later on I saw Mandela alone at Victor Verster Prison. The Polsmoor visit in early September 1987 was particularly interesting because we had communion with him. The chief military chaplain, an Afrikaner, was with us and he seemed a bit unhappy and uncomfortable. But Mandela warmly invited him to join us and we all had holy communion together. It was very moving and memorable.

'At the inauguration of President Mandela at Union Buildings in May 1994, I also saw the warders we had seen that time in Polsmoor Prison. One of them had served us with a meal in the prison and here they were, the captors, invited by Prisoner Mandela to his presidential inauguration! South Africa is a very strange place and full of its own special miracles!'

To recount a mere fraction of what was done by other church leaders and Christian organisations is impossible, in terms of doing justice to the saga. But one other merits mention as typical of work done by so many clergy, especially blacks.

I'm thinking of the Rev. Dr Khoza Mgojo, a Harvard PhD in Hebrew, Greek and Semitic languages, and for years a Methodist Church leader. Since 1990 he has been President of the South African Council of Churches on whose role he commented: 'The main contribution of the SACC to the struggle has been to stand for the truth. When all the organisations were banned, a vacuum was left and the SACC took up the position of the organisations. The background was always there of the church challenging the government. In fact, between 1990 and 1994 we spent endless time meeting the government and cabinet ministers.

'But we also had to get all our concerns to grassroots. That is when I decided to leave theological education and go into the pastorate in Umlazi, a black township near Durban. But this was very hard because of the intensifying violent confrontation between ANC and IFP. So I spent most of my time comforting the bereaved from both camps. In fact I started a Sunday service in a church broken down and ransacked by the violence. People started to come back.

'But my life seemed to be one of constant funerals. It was terrible. For example, at Folweni there was a young man who had had nine members of his family killed. They started with the father, then the mother and right down to the youngest, but he had somehow managed to escape. I was called to minister to this young man and believe it or not, he is now a key member of my church and has no bitterness in his heart. This is a miracle of the Gospel and we have seen many miracles like this.'

Election Preparation

As the elections drew nearer in 1993 and into 1994, Khoza and hundreds of other pastors and groups also got involved extensively in voter education.

The fact was that because the majority of the population were voting for the first time and education about democracy was virtually nonexistent, an enormous amount of work had to be done to ensure that people voted in an informed way.

Many Christian groups worked on this alongside sterling work done by Judge Kriegler and the IEC. The list includes Caesar Molebatsi's Youth Alive group in Soweto, Fano Sibisi's Christians for Truth at Kwasisabantu, Black Sash, the Institute for Contextual Theology, the SACC, the YWCA, the Southern African Catholic Bishops' Conference, Lawyers for Human Rights, IDASA, Matla Trust, the Independent Forum for Electoral Education, Independent Mediation Services of South Africa, the Institute for Multi-Party Democracy, the Centre for Development Studies, and many others.

Father Tim Smith, a Catholic priest and a man of enormous courage, spent seven years at Elandskop near Pietermaritzburg at the height of the violence until he was forced to leave after receiving many death threats. He moved to Soweto, where he later created all sorts of voter education materials, including a series of posters depicting the details of the Government of National Unity and explaining such concepts as the relevance of the regional and national ballot. These were circulated nationally.

Amazing work in this field was also done by Diakonia, directed by Paddy Kearney. Diakonia was founded in 1976 as an agency of the churches in the Durban area to work on issues of justice and social change. Not surprisingly, therefore, it was they who organised the KwaZulu-Natal churches campaign, 'Educate for Democracy', headed by Ntomb'futhi Zondo and launched in April 1993 by Roman Catholic Archbishop Wilfrid Napier.

The Natal Church Leaders' Group asked the campaign committee to act for them in planning and running four information days for church leaders, clergy and lay leaders in various parts of Natal. These were successful in getting up-to-date information on the electoral system to about 250 other key church leaders.

Diakonia also played a key role in facilitating the drawing up, endorsement and distribution of more than 125,000 copies of the Natal Church Leaders' Group pastoral letter 'Christians, Democracy and the Church' in Zulu, English and Afrikaans. This letter, endorsed by twenty-four key leaders from all parts of Natal, played a significant role in undergirding the campaign to involve Christians fully in democracy education work and electoral preparations.

During the build-up to the elections, therefore, voter workshops through the churches were running at the rate of at least two a week plus input-giving sessions during Sunday services.

In the period leading to the elections, the Pietermaritzburg Agency for Christian Social Awareness (PACSA) also seconded two of their workers, Gcina Hlope and Nhlanhla Radebe, to undertake voter education particularly to farm workers, rural areas and schools. Their human rights researcher, Karen Buckenham, was heavily involved with KwaZulu-Natal Election Observer Network (KNEON) and PACSA's director, Peter Kerchhoff, was seconded to the IEC to head the Pietermaritzburg sub-region. Peter, after a few weeks in which to recover from the intense hard work of basically doing two years' work in four months, described it as 'a most worthwhile experience and such a privilege'.

Their work through the years has been a vital link in keeping the churches informed about what has been happening at grassroots level, especially at the height of the violence in KwaZulu-Natal, of which more anon.

St James Church
Before leaving these many different contributions of Christian witness brought in the years of run-up to the elections, one should not omit the poignant offering of courage and

faith midst shock and suffering which came from St James Church in Kenilworth, Cape Town.

Returning home from a preaching engagement on the evening of 25 July 1993, I turned on the TV and witnessed, along with the rest of our aching nation, the horrendous spectacle of the aftermath of an armed attack by five gunmen on the evening worship service of that church. The church's pastor, Frank Retief, later reported that, when the gunmen burst into the sanctuary, 'bullets raked the congregation'. Then they 'lobbed a hand grenade attached to a tin of nails into the assembly'.

Eleven died horrifically, fifty-three were wounded, some maimed for life. South Africa had seen endless massacres in houses and hostels and, horrifying as they were, this one was different, for it was in a church and during an act of praise and worship. I remember that my wife Carol and I sat stunned as we watched the report in our living room. Was God really going to prove greater than this? First reports suspected those responsible as being from APLA, the armed wing of the PAC, whose leaders we had been meeting during our Kolobe weekends. One did not know what to think.

But in the days which followed, the astonishing testimony emerging from St James revealed an extraordinary measure of forgiveness and lack of bitterness toward the perpetrators, whoever they were.

In his book *Tragedy to Triumph*, written soon after the massacre, Retief noted that the attack on their church had not lasted more than thirty seconds,

> but it was thirty seconds that shook the nation, brought worldwide condemnation of political violence and changed the lives of literally thousands of people for ever. It made us face the deep questions of life. It forced us to confront the mysteries of our existence in this world, the fearsome reality of evil and the massive display of goodwill and sympathy. It forced us to reflect on our view of God

and his relationship to good and evil, and it forced us
to look the world in the face and answer for the things
we believe.[1]

And that look and that answering and that forgiving were
very special contributions to the healing of the land which
was by God's grace tiptoeing over the horizon and into the
hearts of a panting people.

8 Blundering Towards Calamity

Returning violence for violence multiplies violence, adding deeper darkness to a night already devoid of stars.

> Martin Luther King, Jr

South Africa is staring calamity in the face.

> John Kane-Berman

Natalians will determine whether a new political dispensation in South Africa will succeed. If we cannot get our political tolerance right in Natal, we won't achieve success anywhere in the country.

> Robin Carlisle, March 1993

While prayer, faith and witness may have been flourishing in South Africa through these times, the dark underside of our national life often looked as if it was gaining the upper hand. We were, as John Kane-Berman put it in an editorial, 'blundering towards calamity'.

Daily headlines and their stories brought it home and made one's breakfast diet of newspaper with porridge a daily wake-up call to a brooding sense of imminent national catastrophe.

2 JANUARY 1993

Headline: Apla has declared 1993 the 'Year of the Great Storm'

Story: *'Apla's "theatre of war" is expanding daily and covering both urban and rural areas in SA.'*[2]

9 JANUARY
Headline: Unrest clamps on two Natal towns
Story: *'Two strife-torn Natal townships, Bruntville at Mooi River, and Wembezi near Estcourt, have been declared unrest areas . . . in the wake of ongoing violence in the townships.'*[3]

25 JANUARY
Headline: 1992 was 'worst year in history of the SAP'
Story: *'More policemen died violent deaths during 1992 than at any time since the establishment of the South African Police force in 1913.' In 1992 288 policemen died.*[4]

THE MOST VIOLENT SOCIETY ON EARTH

In fact every exposure to the papers, radio or television became a shattering shot to the head and a knock-out blow to the solar plexus. The thing was getting out of hand and we were going down for the count.

We had in fact become one of the most violent societies on earth with our cities the crime capitals of the world. Thus the 1993/94 survey of the South African Institute for Race Relations could record that 'international comparisons showed crime per capita in South Africa to be higher than in other countries for which figures were available'. In the early 1990s the murder rate per 100,000 people in France was four and in the United States it was ten. In South Africa it was ninety-eight. But Natal was the real flashpoint in the country with a murder rate of 213, more than double the rate in the next most violent province.[5]

Human Rights and Religious Freedom

With all this going on and daunting our spirits daily, we felt at African Enterprise that there were also other issues to look at in terms of whatever we could do. We accordingly convened a Consultation of some forty-three Christian leaders and thinkers to look at the issue of human rights and religious freedom from a biblical point of view.

After nearly three days of intense deliberation we reached a set of basic affirmations and convictions based on the clear understanding that human rights are fundamentally divine in origin. Therefore, these rights are inalienable and it is not the prerogative of government either to grant or withhold them. Government is ordained by God to preserve these rights, to establish justice and to maintain peace and order. All government derives its powers from the just consent of the governed.

Responsibilities and Rights

One cry endlessly and of course rightly heard in South Africa throughout these times was the cry for human rights, but much less audible was any word about their concomitant responsibilities. So we affirmed that 'Such rights and responsibilities can only flourish when society respects the moral law of God and encourages each person's moral and spiritual development.'

Our biggest concern was to see God acknowledged in the constitution so that our nation and the new South Africa did not start seeing itself as autonomous and therefore in a position to grant or withhold human rights. In fact we wanted to see the whole constitution and all its provisions and principles acknowledge that we were under God and to be in submission to Him.

We accordingly sent off our document of affirmations and declaration to the heads of all political parties. We also asked to see them to interpret further its provisions and concerns.

We hardly dared believe that something would come of it.

3 MARCH
Headline: Schoolkids massacred
Story: *Masked attackers surrounded a bakkie ferrying children to school in Table Mountain yesterday and shot dead six pupils aged between nine and nineteen.*[6]

Headline: Natal 'is new SA's crucible'
Story: *'Natalians will determine whether a new political dispensation in South Africa will succeed,' says DP MP Robin Carlisle.*[7]

9 MARCH
Headline: Third ambush in a week
Story: *'In the third ambush in a week, four people died yesterday when gunmen opened fire on a bus carrying eighty passengers from Swayimane to the trial of three people arrested in connection with last week's murder of six children near Table Mountain.'*[8]

Table Mountain
The massacre at Table Mountain, near Pietermaritzburg, of six school children and the maiming of others on the way to school brought new horror to the downward spiral in which we all felt trapped. To knock off some warriors of the opposite camp was bad enough, but to take out innocent, defenceless children was barbaric.

What was it all about? An opportunity to learn more came in mid-March when the invitation came to be part of a delegation of inspection, along with ANC and IFP leaders, plus police brigadiers and military generals, and a large contingent from the media. We were to be taken to Table Mountain and 'the war zone' to see for ourselves what was going on. We were to meet at Oribi Airport in Pietermaritzburg.

Two huge military helicopters were on the tarmac and two large buses outside the terminal for the press contingent. Inside was an array of bigwigs. There, for example, was Harry Gwala, ANC boss in the Natal Midlands, and another graduate of Robben Island with over twenty years of traumatic internment there, plus ANC MPs Rob Haswell and Pierre Cronje. To one side, in animated conversation, were Minister of Law and Order Hernus Kriel, and George Bartlett, Natal leader of the National Party. Another worried cluster of IFP leaders included the stormy Velaphi Ndlovu, eloquent Ben Ngubane, and David Ntombela from the Edendale Valley. The contrast was completed by ribboned police brigadiers and military generals. And of course bucketloads of journalists and cameramen everywhere.

After boarding the choppers, we were told to deplane because of engine trouble. Mechanics worked feverishly. As the party of political heavies finally crossed the airport tarmac I commented: 'I hope you powerful gentlemen will forgive me preaching to you, but do you know that in the helicopter is a crucial, indispensable and vital bolt under the rotor which helicopter pilots call the "Jesus Nut"? And unless it's working, and properly in place, the machine won't fly. Just a little illustration for life. Without the Jesus Nut, none of us can fly. Nor can South Africa!'

They all laughed, especially Harry Gwala, with some probably concealing an inner reflection – 'These damned preachers – never miss an opportunity, do they?'

And so we took off for the 'war zone' swooping low over this hill, circling that valley, pausing to hover here and there over devastated villages and then landing at several sites where indescribable horrors had happened. But the special shock of the day for me was getting an aerial view of mile after mile of abandoned, burned-out and derelict houses, shacks and huts.

Mountain-top after mountain-top, most flat like Table Mountain and rising from exquisite valleys, each with its shining, gleaming stream, chattering on its way to join the mighty Tugela River, revealed its own story of ghostly abandonment. A dog sniffing here and there for a morsel midst the burned-out wreckage of his master's hut, a lone chicken pecking away in a miserably bare mealie patch.

I confess I was stunned. This was the 'out-of-sight war' of which white people knew very little. And what untold human tragedies lay behind each tumbled-down and ransacked relic?

Then we were at the spot where the first ambush and massacres of school children had taken place – allegedly by ANC supporters. We climbed out and walked up the hill. Vivid descriptions followed from military and police.

There was a moment of silence. The sun beat down on us. A cow's melancholy moan came over the hill from somewhere.

On impulse I called out: 'Folk, I'd like to say a prayer right here, right now, for these people, for peace in South Africa and for us.'

And I did, calling on God, who alone has the power, to rescue us from these horrors. A few overseas journalists looked distinctly uncomfortable. The South African ones took it all in their stride. But then that's South Africa, a place where God is in fact allowed to feature midst all man's madness.

Another stop followed at a spot allegedly of another ANC ambush. Gwala was justifiably furious when the excuse was given of 'no time' to stop at yet another killing field – this time where IFP were allegedly the perpetrators.

Back at the Imperial Hotel in Pietermaritzburg for a press conference and further briefing, the sparks flew in charge and counter-charge. Not very helpful or edifying. ANC supporters had mobbed by the hundreds, maybe thousands, into the street outside the hotel to present a petition to Minister Kriel. Kriel seemed very beleaguered and I felt for him too as he finally faced the throng outside and called for peace. In fact one could feel for everyone in this awful business. And where blame finally lay for the KwaZulu killing fields was ultimately anybody's guess.

MANDELA

Next day a message came that Harry Gwala wanted me to meet Nelson Mandela the following day.

Billy Graham had given me a leather-bound and inscribed copy of his book *Peace with God* to give Dr Mandela when I could do so personally. Perhaps this was the moment I had been waiting for. My previous two encounters had not allowed this. As I was ushered past all the Pietermaritzburg big shots into the presence of the great man, it was heartwarming to be greeted graciously by first name and to sense that presidential presence, even then, which is part of Nelson Mandela.

'You know, I have been much touched by the messages of Billy Graham which I saw on TV in prison,' he said as I handed him the book. 'Do you know he has preached some of the most inspiring sermons in the world?'

Yes, I knew that!

Mandela then went on to share how he had been a Sunday School teacher in his younger years, and then in prison had hardly ever missed a service, 'of any denomination'.

'The only time I felt any reservation', he went on, 'was when I first went into the NGK service. The dominie was very anxious and nervous. But one day I had a guava which I had saved from my prison meal and I gave it to the dominie to give his wife as a present from me. That really seemed to touch him and we became firm friends. But then the authorities sensed this friendship developing and removed him, so that I never saw him again. It was very sad. A sign of the inhumanity of the system.'

Mandela added that 'going to church now is very difficult for me for several reasons'.

Aides in due time interrupted our conversation with the suddenness of officialdom saying: 'Now that's that for now,' and there was no time to close in prayer. But it had been a fine and memorable experience.

Mandela seemed delighted with the book.

22 MARCH
Headline: PAC, AZAPO to keep fighting
Story: '*At rallies to commemorate Sharpeville Day yesterday, PAC and AZAPO spokesmen made it clear the armed struggle will continue.*'[9]

The ups, the downs. On and on they went. With more downs than ups.

Seeing Through the Gloom

Thus three days after the 22 March headline, journalist Allister Sparks sought to lift the national spirit with his widely syndicated column. His article was headlined 'Seeing through the Gloom' and opened: 'Nations, like individuals, are prone to moods of depression. Moments of collective pessimism prevail when all you hear are the sounds of gloom and cynicism and anyone who ventures a word of hope is looked at as if he is mad.'[10]

Many indeed felt that having hope in South Africa was a sign of either political illiteracy or, if one was politically aware, of incipient dementia. After all, as he noted, there were so many reasons for the mood of depression. 'There is the violence, the crime, the collapse of policing, ministerial incompetence, the lack of political vision anywhere, the seemingly endless cycle of corruption and rising taxes, the unemployment and the uncertainty. Particularly the uncertainty.'[11]

Sparks was articulating widely held feelings of doom and gloom. Not many grasped, as he went on, that 'When a nation is in such a mood of depression it wallows in it. It does not count its blessings, of which we have many.'

But, as Sparks added: 'We have amazing people. People

who at almost every level of our society have struggled with big issues and been strengthened morally and intellectually by that experience. Among them I count a president who, for all his manifold faults, has turned turtle on the whole ideology he was nurtured and raised and came to power in. But in particular I count a string of black political leaders who, after being hounded and abused and out-lawed nearly all their adult lives, after being imprisoned for an unconscionable number of years during which they saw their families harassed and their friends tortured and assassinated, have emerged in the evening of their lives not as bitter people but as conciliators.'[12]

But how could the spirit of conciliation prevail, when neither April nor the normally merry month of May could bring any reprieve to one's breakfast blues?

10 APRIL
Headline: Chris Hani assassinated.

15 APRIL
Headline: SA's day of Anger
Story: *In the wake of Chris Hani's assassination, 'South Africa reeled under the largest labour stayaway in the country's history yesterday but it went horribly wrong in some major city centres. At least five people died and about 300 people were injured.'*[13]

17 APRIL
Headline: Rolling Mass Action
Story: *'South Africa's political crisis in the wake of Chris Hani's murder has deepened further with the announcement of six weeks' rolling mass action by the ANC, and sharp criticism from the government.'*

21 APRIL
Editorial headline: On the brink of anarchy[14]

8 MAY
Headline: Volksfront says no to talks[15]

'Here's some good news, darling,' I said to Carol at breakfast on Monday, 10 May, still 1993.

Headline: Hundreds commit to peace at rally
Story: *Representatives of the ANC, Inkatha, SAP and clergy attended a Pietermaritzburg City Hall rally organised by Pastor Dennis Charles of Team Ministries. 'Several groups left the meeting and took up positions around the city to pray for peace.'*[16]

'That's wonderful,' she replied, trying to smile with all the air of a drowning person clutching at a piece of driftwood.

That was how people felt in those days.

But three days later, even the buoyant Allister Sparks was down. 'Time is running out' headlined his article.[17] On 16 May it was announced that infuriated IFP supporters were marching in protest on Pietermaritzburg, Ixopo and Durban.

One of the realities we were seeing more and more was that there was a failure in the nation to understand accurately the feelings and the dangerously intensifying emotions of the Inkatha Zulus. The problem seemed to lie in the fallacious view among many that KwaZulu was simply another artificial apartheid creation, an anachronistic Bantustan and tribal relic run by a Pretoria surrogate with no popular support. All therefore that was required was to tighten the political thumbscrews and if that failed entertain the notion of the so-called military solution. This would silence what one opposition camp leader called 'the howling dogs of Ulundi'. KwaZulu and Inkatha and the so-called Zulu problem were basically an over-inflated political bubble, pumped up by Pretoria and Zulu traditionalism, which, once popped, would evaporate into the ideologically thin air whence it came.

My own fears of this perception were deep, for I saw it as not only erroneous but thoroughly dangerous. Sidelining or marginalising the IFP, as seemed to be happening, or giving them grounds to disown the developing shape of the new order, could only intensify rage, exacerbate wounded pride, and feed that kind of sectional nationalism which thrives on threats to identity. Such things could produce wounded buffaloes.

In fact my sense was that the IFP Zulus were increasingly feeling, in addition to being humiliated, that their very survival was at stake. One article later quoted King Goodwill Zwelithini saying to the then President de Klerk: 'Can you imagine the hurt that you, as head of state, have inflicted on us Zulus, Mr President, in allowing us to be humiliated in this way, by people who have never conquered us in any war? People who would never conquer us if we were to engage in any such conflict?'[18]

The spirit of conflict was becoming the air we breathed. Where would it all end?

15 JUNE
Headline: Watch your back in Wembezi
Story: *'From December to June this year not a day passed without murder, attempted murder, necklacing, houses being burned, assaults, hand grenade and petrol bomb attacks.'*[19]

25 JUNE
Headline: AWB attacks World Trade Centre

2 JULY
Election date finalised. IFP, KwaZulu government and Conservative Party representatives walk out of talks.

5 JULY
Headline: Eleven die in weekend violence
Story: *'More than 110 people have fled the Ncalu township, outside Ixopo, since an arson attack last week.'*[20]

12 JULY
King Goodwill Zwelithini addresses King's Park rally
and calls for acceptance of KwaZulu under constitution
endorsed by people of KwaZulu-Natal before elections
go ahead.

25 JULY
Attack on St James Church in Kenilworth, Cape Town.
Eleven dead, more than fifty injured.

Little People

The little villages. And the little people. These were among
the main sufferers. Everyone said that Ncalu, an ANC
stronghold, and Maweni, an IFP base, both little villages
near Ixopo in Natal, had become ghost towns. Reported
the *Natal Witness*: 'The two villages are separated by a river
and the two communities had been living peacefully for
generations. About thirty-two women and children from
Ncalu have sought refuge in a church in Ixopo, while the
Natal Witness team found 109 others sheltered in a church
in Umzimkhulu.'[21]
   Yes, the children. One of the most devastating effects
of the violence was the number of homeless children left
to fend for themselves on the streets of our cities and
towns. A friend told me of one young Imbali lad she
had become friends with, Dumisani by name. He had
witnessed one night the horror of the killing of his father
and brothers before managing to escape as his home went
up in flames. The terror and trauma were too much for his
mother, the only other family member to have survived,
and she went insane. Dumisani, now aged ten, is living on
the streets carrying with him emotional scars too deep to
comprehend.
   What will become of him? And of so many other
victims?
   One was thankful for groups like PACSA, which

were so strongly involved with victims of violence and working within crisis situations. For example, during Pietermaritzburg's 'Seven Day War' (25–31 March 1990), in which hundreds were killed and many more displaced, PACSA was working alongside about thirty-six different organisations which had come together. They were helping arrange mass funerals, and minister to the many people rendered homeless. They were working especially with churches in those townships caught in particularly brutal violence.

And what, they must have asked, as did all of us, if these masses of micro conflicts, like Ncalu and Maweni and Imbali, become macro?

It could happen.

25 AUGUST

American student, Amy Biehl, killed in Gugulethu township. She was to have returned home to California two days later.

4 SEPTEMBER

Conservative Party leader Ferdi Hartzenberg threatens civil war if Transitional Executive Council (TEC) is implemented.

23 SEPTEMBER

TEC Bill passed in Parliament. Conservative Party walks out of Parliament for the rest of the session.

Albie Sachs

Yes, it could become macro. Everyone was feeling it. But September brought forth one ray of sunlight for some of us. Just when we had concluded that our document and presentation from the February Consultation on Human Rights and Religious Freedom had gone the way of all flesh, a letter reached me from Nelson Mandela, saying he wanted us to take up the matter with Albie Sachs, member of the ANC's Constitutional Committee, and some of his colleagues.

In next to no time, four of us from our consultation were in Cape Town with Albie Sachs and a couple of his fellow committee members. Our little cluster was Ron Steele (right-hand man to Rhema Bible Church leader, Ray McCauley), Gerald Pillay (a University of South Africa theology professor), his wife Nirmala (a scholar, author and human rights specialist) and myself. We wondered if we were going to get anywhere.

We had all heard of the celebrated Albie Sachs who had had his right arm blown off in Mozambique, allegedly by the South African dirty tricks brigade. Some said he was a communist. Others that he was an atheist. To conservative whites he was one of the bad boys. What could we get from him in terms of a recognition of God in the constitution?

All of us were unprepared for the graciousness and charm with which he received us and listened to us. Soft spoken, with a wry smile and the self-assurance of one who could see his ship coming into harbour and his cause being vindicated, he followed us with rapt attention.

'God at the beginning of the constitution,' we suggested. 'Yes. And maybe a prayer, something like Nkosi Sikelel'i-Afrika at the end,' he added. 'I don't see why not. After all, the great majority of people in this country are religious and God-fearing. I'll send this to our senior ANC leadership in Johannesburg.' We then worked on some wording.

Finally with a gracious farewell and left-handed handshake, he left the room leaving the four of us sitting there mildly stunned.

It seemed too good to be true. But would anything more come of it? We wondered.

9 OCTOBER
SADF raids APLA safe house in Transkei; five killed.

14 OCTOBER

Polish immigrant Jacob Waluz, and former Member of Parliament Clive Derby-Lewis found guilty of Chris Hani's murder.

15 OCTOBER

Mandela and de Klerk win Nobel Peace Prize.

Waluz and Derby–Lewis sentenced to death.

21 OCTOBER

Headline: Dozens die in tribal battle

Story: *'A clash between two rival factions in Loskop yesterday morning left twenty-four people dead and five seriously wounded. A hundred huts were also gutted during the fighting.'*[22]

Headline

Afrikaner Volksunie walks out of World Trade Centre talks

4 NOVEMBER

Headline: Blow to peace hopes after priest's murder

Story: *Rev. Richard Kgetsi killed in Port Shepstone was 'well known for mediating in grassroots conflicts between the African National Congress, the Inkatha Freedom Party and security forces'.*[23]

9 NOVEMBER

Headline: Six shot dead in Ixopo

Story: *'Six people, including a 70-year-old woman and children aged three and four, were killed in Ixopo on Sunday, bringing to eighteen the number of people killed at the weekend in the midlands region.'*[24]

10 NOVEMBER

Headline: New Risk

Story: '*The Freedom Alliance could pose a security risk to the new South Africa,*' *President F.W. de Klerk said yesterday.*[25]

Midst all of this, the multiparty talks pressed forward relentlessly at the World Trade Centre. For better or worse a new interim constitution was going to come about regardless.

A NATION UNDER GOD

Almost on impulse I decided to go up with my colleague Peter Kerton-Johnson to the World Trade Centre on Friday, 12 November. It turned out to be a fascinating day.

The most rewarding of many encounters was with Albie Sachs. When we arrived at the Trade Centre, we saw the 8 November version of the constitution and were very disappointed to find nothing in the preamble in terms of what we had hoped for. When we met Mr Sachs, however, he said: 'Have you seen the fruits of your labours?' We looked somewhat blank. The 8 November version of the constitution had had nothing of God in the preamble.

'No,' he said, 'I'm talking about the latest version, dated today, 12 November.' This he produced from his briefcase.

And there to our total delight was the preamble which opened: 'In humble submission to Almighty God, we the people of South Africa declare that . . .' etc., etc. Then at the very end of the constitution is the prayer 'Nkosi sikilel'i-Afrika' – 'God bless Africa' in six languages. God at the beginning and God at the end of South Africa's new draft constitution.

Our hearts absolutely rejoiced as we believed this to be important and fundamental. There just has to be a final, divine and absolute court of appeal above the combined labours and corporate human wisdom of human beings.

Atmosphere

A week later, on 17 November, the interim constitution was to be finalised and signed. It was not a day to miss. So back to Johannesburg.

Nothing could dampen the extraordinary feeling of excitement in the air. Everyone was aware that this was an historic moment as the old order died. The country was being 'born again' in a remarkable way.

It was a long wait and at times the whole process looked in danger of aborting.

My journal records the exhausting but never-to-be-forgotten night.

'The final and closing plenary, instead of beginning at 2 p.m, as we anticipated, finally began at 11 p.m. The whole thing was extraordinary and one has to say once again that one could not but admire all that has gone on in this process, even though there are 'warts and all' components.'

Negatives

'As the process moved forward during the night in terms of approving the constitution, the sustained negative and "reservation or rejection" voices came, curiously enough, from both the AVU and the PAC, although of course for very different reasons. But it was nevertheless an extraordinary and moving moment when the new constitution was in fact finally approved at 12.14 a.m. to the bleary-eyed but generally approving delegates and assembly. The constitutional instrument, I suspect, is far from perfect. But it is in the circumstances, and with all the political intricacies given, the best thing the country could come up with at this time and everybody must now work at it and get on with the job of building the new South Africa creatively and positively.'

On one of my 'refreshment breaks', my journal reminds

me of meeting President de Klerk, 'likewise taking a breather from the proceedings. Had a very good ten minutes with the President. He said: "It is really amazing to be having a revolution without a revolution" by which he meant a total change in the social order without the thing taking place violently. He felt it was a very great achievement in the whole negotiating process that a deal had been struck that was not a "winner-take-all" solution at the next election. But rather a *regstaat* (a state under constitutional regulation) has emerged. In this the constitution and the rule of law are supreme above the domination of one party.

'After the finalising and approving of the constitution, there then began a daunting catalogue of twenty-one speeches by twenty-one political party heads!

'The proceedings finally wound up with a powerful statement at about 3.30 a.m. from Justice Mohamed who noted that: "As the jailer and the jailed of yesterday took the first faltering steps in February 1990 with their pledges for a new day, so as they then pledged, we have now today redeemed that pledge, if not totally, at least substantially. In consequence our nation will awake in a few hours to the promise of a new dawn."

'As we all staggered to our feet, I think the realisation of the historic was indelibly etched upon our souls. Mandela moved out of the auditorium almost trampled underfoot by a barrage of press and security people. He must have felt twenty-seven years in prison had been worth it if thereby he could finally have been brought to this moment.'

But, don't forget, the IFP Zulus were still out in the cold.

7 DECEMBER
Headline: We'll go ahead without Freedom Alliance
Sub-headline: Government and ANC talks with Alliance collapse.
Story: '*Eleventh hour attempts to get Inkatha and the*

Freedom Alliance (FA) on board a political settlement collapsed yesterday with little prospect of rescue.'[26]

11 DECEMBER
Headline: Leaders a 'shining example'
Story: *F. W. de Klerk and Nelson Mandela receive their Nobel Peace Prizes in Oslo, Norway. De Klerk said, 'The driving force for change in South Africa was a process "of introspection, of soul-searching, of repentance".'*[27]

14 DECEMBER
Headline: FA [Freedom Alliance] demands cause stalemate
Sub-headline: IFP to boycott polls.
Story: *'The Inkatha Freedom Party is to campaign for a boycott of next year's elections, IFP political director Ziba Jiyane said yesterday.'*[28]

16 DECEMBER
Headline: Nine Natal police killed
Story: *'Another two policemen have died in Natal and three others have been attacked. The latest deaths bring to nine the number of Natal policemen killed in the past week. So far this year, 239 policemen have been killed countrywide.'*[29]

17 DECEMBER
Headline: Defend KwaZulu with your lives
Sub-headline: King, Buthelezi demand that Zulus rule themselves.[30]

18 DECEMBER
Headline: 127 murders in a week
Sub-headline: Natal in grip of pre-Christmas crime wave.[31]

21 DECEMBER
Headline: Last-ditch talks fail

Story: '*A bruising ten-hour meeting between the govern-ment, ANC and Freedom Alliance failed to find an inclusive political settlement last night.*'[32]

22 DECEMBER
Headline: Late deal keeps door open[33]

23 DECEMBER
Headline: 'Over the threshold' to new era
Sub-headline: Curtain falls on white Parliament.[34]

28 DECEMBER
Headline: Christmas weekend among the bloodiest
Story: '*At least twenty-four people were murdered in Natal on Christmas Day, bringing to forty-four the number of people killed in the province since Thursday.*'[35]

It seemed that in spite of constitutional breakthroughs and touches of euphoria here and there, events in KwaZulu-Natal could still take us over the cliff. Interim constitution and all, the language of civil war was nevertheless every-where in the air.

Thus with the sun struggling to rise on a new day, the darkness persisted and we found ourselves, in spite of everything, still blundering towards calamity.

End-of-the-year statistics told the story. Nearly half of all political violence fatalities were in KwaZulu-Natal. And the graph was upwardly mobile.

'Peter,' I said to my AE colleague just before going away on leave, 'let's fax a stack of KwaZulu-Natal leaders and call for a KwaZulu-Natal Leaders' Forum, early next year. We need to stress that if KwaZulu-Natal unravels, the whole nation will unravel.'

That was now very clear. KwaZulu-Natal was the key.

Part Two

MIRACLE MOMENTS

9 The Man of My Counsel

The choice is ours. But before long that choice could
slip through our fingers and we could find ourselves
powerless, the victims of a frightening, destructive
power, like that of an earthquake.
> Bishop Stanley Mogoba, February 1994

I believe in providential intervention.
> Professor Washington Okumu

The atmosphere was laden with foreboding as 1994 began.
More than three hundred and fifty people in Kwazulu-
Natal had died as a result of political violence in the first few
weeks of the year; this represented some 60 per cent of all
such deaths nationwide. The negotiation crisis at top level
was deepening with neither the Afrikaner Conservatives
nor the IFP anywhere near participating in the election act.
Said the *Natal Witness* on 11 February: 'The negotiations
crisis deepened last night when the white right wing said
they would reject the election and its result and Inkatha
declared that without a settlement in the talks, it would not
register for the election.' On 12 February, the IFP Central
Committee decided finally and officially not to participate
in the elections.

Voter education efforts were becoming virtually
impossible to conduct in many townships and in much
of Northern KwaZulu-Natal. At a luncheon for Indian
pastors in Chatsworth several told us that their parishioners

were being constantly terrified by threats from some blacks with inflated expectations of what the election would bring. One Indian housewife returned from a day in Durban to find her gardener painting her house green.

'What on earth are you doing?' she protested.

'I prefer green walls, madam. Because this is going to be my house after the elections.'

Others came to homes in Chatsworth and said: 'Here's one rand. It's a deposit on your house which I'm coming for on 30 April.'

A large American multinational company in South Africa issued a decree forbidding any of its US-based personnel to enter the country for a month before or after the election period. 'They knew that anything could happen. No chances could be taken,' said Johannesburg businessman Owen Hooker.

We also heard that one of the world's top international news photographers was being moved from Bosnia to KwaZulu-Natal 'as it would be the world's next major trouble spot'.

In the wider nation some people were near panic. For example in Pretoria, and in many other places, shop shelves were stripped bare and tinned foods sold out as people stockpiled fearing some kind of siege situation. One store bought a million candles in anticipation of an electrical blackout by sabotage. The Hendrick Verwoerd Hospital in Pretoria, a fortnight before the election, was anticipating and preparing for 3,000 casualties on Inauguration Day.

KwaZulu-Natal Leaders' Forum

With these things in the air and with negotiations seemingly irrevocably broken down, it is not surprising that there was an atmosphere of doom and gloom when the KwaZulu-Natal Leaders' Forum met at the Royal Hotel in Durban on Thursday, 24 February.

Very senior people from across the political, professional, business and church spectrum were there – provincial party heads, corporate bosses, numerous MPs, and several bishops. Roman Catholic Archbishop Wilfrid Napier was our chairperson.

An assortment of keynote addresses, panels and discussion times made up the day.[1] From all came the sense of urgency. Said Khoza Mgojo in the opening devotional: 'Everyone knows our country and province are in danger from forces of alienation and violence which are threatening to break us apart.'

In my own comments, I observed: 'We are meeting at a terrific moment in the history of our nation and of our province. We know that, both around the world and the country, all eyes in many ways are on Natal with a mix of anxiety, anticipation, despair, fear and fascination.'

Observed Stanley Mogoba: 'History is presenting us with a unique opportunity to make choices and to effect changes in our country. If we miss this opportunity we may well find that the only task left to us is to comfort the bereaved and bury the dead.'

Business leader Tony Ardington noted that 'business people fear the economic consequences of exclusion of KwaZulu-Natal from the election process and would wish the leaders to meet together to resolve the issues that make it impossible to hold free and fair elections.'

Natal ANC leader Jacob Zuma was succinct: 'Our country has been polarised.'

As the day ended, Wilfrid Napier boldly asked all to stand, link hands and sing, yes sing, the Lord's Prayer! Three major resolutions were before us. The first was to give impetus and encouragement to the meeting of Nelson Mandela and Mangosuthu Buthelezi, planned for the following Tuesday, and brokered by Durban businessman Arnold Zulman. Second, there was encouragement for Christian leaders, wherever possible, to give backstage facilitation to deepened encounters between political leaders on different sides of the equation. Third, there was an implicit and sometimes explicit call for Christians across KwaZulu-Natal to rise at this zero hour and make a greater contribution as peacemakers across the province in its hour of mounting peril.

Commented Elsie Buthelezi, a cousin of the Chief Minister, afterwards: 'It was remarkable as we left the hotel hearing people say: "Praise God that we came here, because now we really know what is happening in KwaZulu-Natal." It was so important to clear the confusion from the minds of people.'

The day after the forum, we shared some of its results and ideas were shared with a large group of Durban pastors at a breakfast meeting. Afterwards in a more intimate and very small cluster (the Durban Task Force) we said: 'What about calling together Christian people from all over KwaZulu-Natal to King's Park Stadium – say on Sunday, 17 April, ten days before the seemingly impossible election?' For some of us God's word in Joel 2:15–18 became not only a decisive mandate to be obeyed, but a great act of faith to be embarked upon. Could it be that if we acted in faith on this and obeyed, and called Christian people together for a solemn act of assembly, repentance and prayer, God Himself would act supernaturally to intervene and save South Africa at even this later-than-midnight hour?

To be sure, command, condition and promised outcome were there. The words of Joel began to ring in our souls like a clarion call: 'Blow the trumpet . . . declare a holy fast, call a sacred assembly. Gather the people, consecrate the assembly; bring together the elders, gather the children . . . Let the priests, who minister before the Lord, weep . . . [and] say, "Spare your people, O Lord" . . . Then the Lord will be jealous for his land and take pity on his people.'

As we began to share the call around the province the idea took wings. We were on a thermal. And it had to be, we felt, the 'Jesus Peace Rally'. It couldn't be the Combined Churches Rally or an Interfaith rally or something like that. It had to be the *Jesus* Peace Rally. It had to be named with the Name that is above every name, with the Name of the One who could say: 'All power in heaven and on earth is committed to me.' Yes, only One with that sort of power could help us now. Otherwise we were lost.

Methodist Bishop Norman Hudson wonderfully and ably chaired the Jesus Peace Rally committee, made up of church leaders from all across Durban. To AE's hustling, bustling and indefatigable Singaporean, the Rev. Soh Chye Ann, we gave the superhuman task of co-ordinating the exercise.

Would 30 come? Or 300? Or 3,000? We were not to know. The job was to obey. And to rustle up ever more prayer and intercession for South Africa both in the country and overseas. That at least was clear.

INTERNATIONAL MEDIATION

On Tuesday, 1 March, the meeting between Mandela and Buthelezi produced a very encouraging agreement to pursue international mediation as a means to solve their differences. This endeavour would also explore whether there was any way left whereby, with only eight weeks to go, the IFP could enter the election.

A week or so later in a seemingly chance meeting with IFP National Chairman Frank Mdlalose at the World Trade Centre, I asked if the list of mediators was finalised, as we had some ideas which we had not yet got round to presenting.

'No, brother, the list is not finalised. Send your ideas. Quickly.'

The next forty-eight hours were one long and frantic flurry of phone calls around the world to Christian linkages at such places as the UN in New York, to aides of former US President Jimmy Carter at the Carter Center in Atlanta and to Tom Getman of World Vision. Getman was travelling with former US Secretary of State James Baker in the Middle East and Western Europe.

We also sought out constitutional experts in the UK, Europe, Australia, West Africa and Kenya. It seemed vital to include veteran Kenyan diplomat Professor Washington Okumu whom we had got to know some years previously in the Newick Park Initiative, which had brought together international Christian diplomats from the US, Europe and Africa, including business and political leaders of all shades of political opinion in South Africa.

Okumu had been involved in the affairs of Southern Africa for at least twenty years, having been tied in with the advance work for the settlement of the Rhodesia crisis in the late 1970s as well as in the run-up to CODESA I in South Africa. He knew and was highly respected by both Mandela and Buthelezi. And besides, as we later discovered, the President of Tanzania had long been urging him to come to South Africa to make a contribution in the present crisis. Moreover, while at Harvard University, he had studied under, and was thus quite familiar with, Henry Kissinger.

As our unfinished draft list was submitted by fax to both national and provincial leadership of the ANC, IFP and government, I phoned Okumu in Nairobi and urged him to consider coming to South Africa to be a part of the mediation team.

'But what about the security problem in South Africa and Natal right now?' he asked one night on the telephone.

'Brother,' I teased him, 'Sadat went to Jerusalem, so you can come to Natal!'

'Come now,' he replied with a twinkle, 'I'm not sure I like that analogy when you consider what eventually happened to Sadat!'

He said he'd pray about it, but sounded rather reluctant about the idea.

James Baker with his vast international and diplomatic experience gave urgency via Tom Getman to direct an appeal to the critical parties. Mr Baker said in a very heartfelt letter which reached South African leaders that 'you could see the loss of a million lives'. Baker's compelling letter of concern included the reflection that healing from the American Civil War took at least a hundred years because once internecine war is under way, other extreme diabolical forces are let loose which are beyond the control of mere mortals. Working on seemingly intractable problems in such places as the Middle East and Southern Africa for so many years, he would have known.

Some days later, we learned that the ANC and IFP had finalised their team of international mediators. It was to be led by Dr Henry Kissinger and Lord Carrington, former UK Foreign Secretary. None of the people from our list had been selected.

To my horror, and no doubt that of many others, there was no African presence. It seemed utterly absurd, we thought, considering that South Africa is a uniquely African rather than a Western problem. With respect, how could Kissinger and Carrington and Co. possibly grasp its intricate and very local dimensions?

It was time to urge Washington Okumu to come anyway. To his enormous credit and with courage and faith he agreed. This coincided with other urgings from African leaders in other parts of the continent. A Christian lady in Kenya quickly helped him get finance and tickets together.

Meantime, over the 11–13 March weekend, the Freedom Alliance fell apart and Bophuthatswana came adrift at the seams midst general chaos leading to a takeover of the territory by the Transitional Executive Council (TEC) and the South African government.

In the press on 14 March, SACP leader Joe Slovo commented ominously: 'One down, two to go', the other two being Ciskei and KwaZulu. My blood ran cold. The Boputhatswana way would not work in KwaZulu, that was for sure.

Said Frank Mdlalose over the phone the following day: 'Brother, we know what is next and what is coming. It will be so unfortunate.' We prayed together and signed off.

For myself, there was only the sense of desperation. These had been days of expending huge energies on behalf of this process, and certainly without the Lord one would have felt absolutely hopeless about the prospects. But who was to know? Maybe He would pluck some miracle brand from the burning.

We heard later that the ANC had taken over the magisterial offices of Umlazi, near Durban, taken down the KwaZulu and South African flags and raised the ANC flag. The township was apparently sealed off and people could not come in and out. This was really very serious.

The good news was that all signs relating to the Jesus Peace Rally were looking positive. My journal records: 'The Lord must do a great and mighty thing. Maybe only He now can raise up a standard that will prevent this place catching fire.'

Thursday, 17 March brought more depression out of an early morning phone conversation with Frank Mdlalose. What was depressing was Dr Frank's insistence that the issue of the election was a dead one because for IFP the cut-off points and deadlines had been passed. Now the only question for mediation was the final shape of the South African constitution. That was now the battlefront, not the issue of whether IFP would or would not come into the elections. That had been settled in the negative.

Frank too was in despair.

In closing, I reminded him of Churchill's most famous and shortest speech ever. It was to the schoolboys at Harrow: 'Never give up, never give up, never give up, never, never, never!' Then Churchill had sat down.

After a meeting in Durban the next day, called by the

ANC for religious leaders of various faiths, we stepped into the afternoon sunlight to see papers and posters with the banner headlines: 'Zulu Kingdom Proclaimed'. It announced that the Zulu King had declared KwaZulu a sovereign independent kingdom and was calling on Zulus to defend their fatherland with their blood and make whatever sacrifices were necessary.

'The King is throwing down the gauntlet,' said a Zulu friend to me as we drove to Pietermaritzburg. Things were reaching boiling point.

IDASA's Paul Graham phoned next day, quite desperate. Were there no cards left to play in Ulundi? 'The clock is ticking,' he lamented, 'there are five weeks to go, and as of now we cannot see how the election can take place in KwaZulu-Natal. Only 40 per cent of the polling stations can be secured at this time. The rest are in no-go areas.'

Paul felt both sides were moving towards options neither of them wanted, but from which neither could extract itself. Rather like going down a slippery slope towards a precipice. The one option before the authorities was to postpone the election, in which case the country would blow up, especially via the explosively impatient black youth in the townships. Yet if the election went ahead as planned, Natal would blow. Paul was about as concerned and despairing as anyone I had heard in a long while. And he is one of those people who makes molehills out of mountains.

We needed a huge miracle.

Weighty Moment

Oh yes, one mighty moment for me came on Wednesday, 23 March. Says my journal: 'I went to my weekly WeighLess weigh-in and, what a lucky boy I was, and a good one, no less, because I got a star! That means I achieved 10kg of weight loss and thus had only 0.4kg to go to reach my goal weight of 90kg. One of the local fatties at Hilton seemed fairly unimpressed and with mock seriousness said: "But you are a man!" As if to say one of the properties of men is that they can cheat on WeighLess and yet lose weight! Oh well, that's the luck of the bounce, I suppose.

Or was it just the election?!

Okumu Arrives

Meanwhile Washington Okumu, though coming on his own initiative and in a personal capacity, had gone to Harare to secure the informal blessing of Zimbabwean President Robert Mugabe and the Organisation of African Unity of whose Southern African Committee Mugabe was Chairman. President Hosni Mubarak of Egypt, OAU Chairman, had chaired a special OAU ad-hoc committee on South Africa in Harare which Okumu attended in a private capacity in order to brief the African leaders and urge them to do something about the unfolding crisis in South Africa, But unfortunately not much came out of that Harare meeting.

We faxed Chief Minister Buthelezi on 27 March about the planned arrival next day of Professor Okumu and our hope of flying him out to Ulundi on Wednesday, the 28th. In a fax to the Chief I emphasised that 'Okumu comes in the Name of the Lord and in his personal capacity.'

There were just four weeks to go to the elections. A race was on between Christ and catastrophe.

Sunday evening, 27 March, my colleague Peter Kerton-Johnson, who had performed herculean labours on the organisational side to line up a host of meetings for Okumu, met the big Kenyan at Durban Airport.

Next day he began a series of briefing meetings with various leaders from a range of parties across the spectrum, which were to last for four days. Though already something of an expert on South Africa, Okumu listened avidly and registered every nuance of concern or posture or grievance from every side.

Following a superb in-depth time with Dr Ziba Jiyane of the IFP and with DP leaders Mike Ellis and Kobus Jordaan, Okumu was due to meet the ANC's Jacob Zuma at 2 p.m. But this fell through with the awful news that Jacob's house in Northern KwaZulu-Natal had been razed to the ground by arsonists.

Okumu met again, this time alone, with Ziba Jiyane – 'African to African', as he put it – to pursue his desire to understand the IFP position in depth. One of the upshots was that Ziba became convinced then that Okumu should be on the international mediating team.

After this, Okumu was ready to return to Pieter-maritzburg, but the ever tenacious and bull-doggish Peter felt they could make one last try for Jacob at the ANC offices, even though they had been unable to get him during the day. The dear man, with his home burned down, had been in crisis all day and then was headed to Johannesburg that night. By one of those extraordinary workings of the Lord which humans cannot easily put together, Peter broke through officialdom at the ANC offices about 7 p.m. to locate Jacob. He then drove him to the airport, 'as slowly as I could,' said the usually speedy Peter, thus leaving time for Jacob and Okumu to talk together in the car.

Later the professor and I reflected on what the new day would bring forth, and then prayed together that the Lord would open the way to Ulundi. That remained our prayer, although the news said that on Thursday the King, Buthelezi, de Klerk and Mandela were to be meeting. So getting through to Ulundi would be extraordinarily difficult, but we had a charter plane on standby to whisk us out there. 'So, Lord,' I wrote in my journal early next morning, 'we live for today and give you the day knowing that sufficient unto the day is the evil thereof.'

Later that morning Peter and I met with Dutch Reformed leaders, both black and white, about the Jesus Peace Rally. At the end of our sharing on the rally we enquired whether they felt the election should be postponed or could go ahead. Two of the black pastors were from Natal. One said: 'There is no way the election can go ahead without terrible bloodshed.' Said the other: 'If we do not go ahead, the townships throughout the country will explode.' That was about as succinct a description of the country's Catch 22 situation as could be offered. But, against all odds, Frank Mdlalose rang later to say a visit to Ulundi was on.

ULUNDI

Neville McIntosh, director of 'Alpha Air' Charter Company, Pietermaritzburg, woke on Wednesday, 30 March with a sense of excitement, and said to his wife: 'You know, dear, it's very exciting to be part of all this. God is good. I don't know who this is going to Ulundi, but I feel in my spirit it's very important. We must pray for the whole thing and ask the Lord for something from His Word to give them.'

Peter had in fact chartered a little twin-engined plane from McIntosh. Upon arrival at Oribi Airport, we had a beautiful time of prayer about our errand out on the tarmac with the pilot and Neville. Then away we went on the wings of doxology!

It was time for a snack. On each of our trays was a Bible passage from Neville and his wife. One of them (Isa. 46: 10–11) read: 'I am God and there is no other; I am God, and there is none like me. Declaring the end from the beginning and from ancient times things not yet done, saying, "My counsel shall stand, and I will accomplish all my purpose," calling a bird of prey from the east, *the man of my counsel* from a far country.' (My emphasis.)

'The man of my counsel from a far country.' Neville, who knew nothing of Okumu from the far country of Kenya, had seemingly stumbled on to God's purposes and plan being worked out at that moment.

Flying over lovely KwaZulu and its majestic valleys

below, I wrote there and then in the margin of my Bible: 'Lord, let your counsel stand and accomplish your purpose to save a country. And thank you for the man of your counsel from a far country.'

We landed at Ulundi and were whisked to the Parliament buildings and ushered into a rather grand conference room where the Chief Minister was just wrapping up what seemed to have been a very irritating interview with a number of American journalists. He had apparently found them arrogant and omniscient and seemingly it had not been a happy time.

But as Okumu entered the room, the Chief's face lit up and his arms flew heavenward, before a great embrace.

'So, you've come!' he exulted. The sight was of old and trusted friends meeting. Our hearts warmed and took hope.

The lunch discussion was very cordial and gave Okumu further time to put forth various proposals and secure further understandings relating to what the situation called for. It seemed the IFP would want a two-month delay in order to get its election machine running, assuming certain other concessions could be secured. I personally felt that four weeks were the most anybody could ask for, especially from Mandela, who would be put in a very tight spot by the notion of delay.

At the end of our time, Peter, Okumu and I had a precious few moments of prayer with the Chief. At one point he said to us, 'I see the hand of God in all of this.'

'May it be so,' my journal recalls, 'because unless the Lord works out some of the things we are talking about, they will never be.'

We flew back to Pietermaritzburg with lightened hearts and praising spirits in the hopes that a positive contribution, with a potential to bring forth something significant, had taken place.

It was clear that Okumu still enjoyed the confidence and affection of the Chief. And that was important.

Danie Schutte

As we got back to Pietermaritzburg, the indefatigable Peter confirmed that his working of another Kolobe linkage had born fruit. Danie Schutte, then Minister of Home Affairs, would come to my home at 9.30 that night to meet Washington Okumu. Being the government's head honcho on all things electoral, it promised to be a key encounter.

Again there was instant chemistry as Washington Okumu drew Danie out on the situations and problems as he saw them. Danie was even ready to admit that he could not see how the whole election could be pulled off in the time available, and confessed: 'The nine hundred electoral supervisors needed for KwaZulu-Natal are nowhere near in place and we have only four weeks to go. The number of polling stations required will be at least 50 per cent short, because only about 50 per cent are no longer in "no-go" areas.'

When Okumu asked him how ballot papers could be distributed, some eighty million of them, if they would only arrive in the country on 17 April, leaving some six or so working days for distribution, Danie admitted the task seemed hopeless and administratively impossible. We felt deeply with him in his frustration because the problems had been created by the extensive delays. Now the administration of the whole exercise by the IEC had become humanly impossible.

In fact, Danie felt the wheels of the Independent Electoral Commission were perilously close to coming off.

Okumu probed where the government were with both the ANC, the IFP and the King. All the time he was soaking it all in, constantly sifting, weighing, pondering, feeling for solutions and a way through.

He agreed to stay in touch with Danie and with us in the next forty-eight hours while he went through to the ANC leadership in Johannesburg. Danie indicated that if Washington Okumu secured any sort of breakthrough on any front, he would be ready not only to convey that to the President within hours, but to go out to Ulundi in order to try and nail things down from the government side.

There seemed to be only one premise, however, and a hugely insecure one at that, on which any of this could come to anything – and that was if the election could be postponed by four weeks. After all there were now only three and a half weeks to go.

We closed the evening very late with prayer. All seemed to us so hopeless. 'But God . . .'

ANC

Next day, working all his old friendships and linkages, Okumu had an amazing time in Johannesburg meeting most of the senior ANC personnel. The professor thought this 'miraculous', given these people's impossible schedules. He also felt that if there was a real and serious commitment from the IFP to participation and some give and take on both sides, then on the ANC side there could be the remote possibility of an adjustment to the date by perhaps a month. But this was entirely his personal opinion because he found it difficult to see how Mandela could possibly sell this idea to his followers. Okumu said he was faxing five key points to the Chief Minister and Frank Mdlalose.

At which he jumped on his plane and headed for an important appointment with the leaders of the Congo in Brazzaville.

That night I had a dream. Upon a brilliant white screen came the words – 'THE LAST OPPORTUNITY'.

I woke with a start – and took it as from the Lord. Everything assumed new urgency.

ADVISOR TO THE MEDIATORS

Then Okumu heard some really great news. He might be invited by Mandela and Buthelezi to be the official African Advisor to the international mediating process. Now that would be something.

Okumu was pleased, having insisted all along that he must be invited by both leaders. This would be even better than being officially in the rank and file of international mediators. He would become official advisor to them all. I had no doubt they would need him.

Easter Day

Events over the 2–3 April weekend moved quickly. Everywhere. Also for me. By the Lord's mysterious workings and linkages an invitation was suddenly before me to visit His Majesty King Goodwill Zwelithini at his palace in Nongoma. It was time to get input from all round on the position of His Majesty. Danie Schutte shared the government view with the longest fax ever to come into my study. 'I'm billing you for a roll of fax paper!' I told Danie over the phone on Easter Saturday when he too was working from home.

Neville McIntosh and Alpha Air were to the rescue in no time flat and early Easter Sunday I was en route to Nongoma, this time alone.

The Nongoma airstrip was unusable we were told, so please land at Ulundi where a car will collect you. But at Ulundi, there was no car as yet. And time was running out.

'You can't land at Nongoma,' said a palace official after we phoned through. 'It's too dangerous.'

I looked at Dave Solomon, my pilot. 'Do you think we can make it?'

He gave a thumbs up: 'Let's try.'

Dave did not know exactly where the Nongoma airstrip was, but we finally spotted something from the air which looked a little less like mealie patch than what surrounded it. After low-flying the length of it, it all seemed reasonable enough and with both of us thoroughly enjoying the excrcise, we began to descend. Dave skipped over the heads of several cattle, touched down beautifully and taxied to where a car was waiting with three of the King's men. They had been radioed to divert from Ulundi to Nongoma.

After an interminable journey with a carload of true-blue royalist Zulus ('all of us are ready to die for our King and our land') we suddenly turned not into a palace, but into a dilapidated school compound. We saw a classroom filled with hundreds of worshippers from the King's entourage, all celebrating Easter Day.

I was horrified when an aide led me into the packed 'church', having understood this to be a private encounter. But no turning back. Up front, the King beckoned me to stand next to him. My alarm was further compounded moments later when in came a massive TV crew from CNN.

I groaned within. Standing beside the King, I was unavoidably in the direct line of camera fire from the world's widest news network! So much for secrecy.

Half an hour later, His Majesty suddenly stood up, and beckoning, led me out to waiting cars. Thence in a flying cavalcade to the palace for a beautiful and extended time of interchange, and discussion and finally prayer. A friend, Muze Kunene, who was also in the church, accompanied me.

The discussion was splendid with helpful insights emerging also for Washington Okumu, about whose sterling labours I told the King. His Majesty's graciousness, shrewdness and humility were impressive.

On the way back to the plane, my three drivers said they were very concerned about an IFP march we had passed en route to the palace. Apparently someone had been shot, although not fatally. They seemed agitated and were deploring the way political groups toted all these AK47s, etc., while traditional weapons were banned. 'The AK47, you see, has become the new traditional weapon and this is terrible.' They were obviously very anxious about what would happen when we got near the Inkatha march and planned political meeting. The other fellow in the front seat had his own AK47 under the dashboard, 'ready in case anyone gets tricky'!

When we came near the political meeting, now going on in a field, there were stacks of youngsters, self-appointed guards, rushing around in the road adjacent to the field, all carrying revolvers, AK47s or something equally lethal. The looks on their faces and the general mood brought home to me that indeed Northern KwaZulu-Natal, and maybe most of the province, had become a tinder box. The thought of having an election under these circumstances struck me as out of the question. I found myself slowly and reluctantly being confirmed in the view that the elections would indeed have to be postponed a month in order for things to calm down.

'Let de Klerk put one soldier in here,' said my driver menacingly, 'and we will declare war. We are ready.'

That trip out to Nongoma confirmed to my heart the deadly seriousness of our provincial plight. We were indeed, as the dream had said, in 'a last opportunity' situation.

Washington Okumu Again

On 5 April, Okumu indicated by phone from Kenya that he wanted 'very urgently' to come back to South Africa late the next day because, in only twelve available hours, and somewhere in between visits to two African presidents, he wanted to see a range of top brass, so that his input could be included in the summit meeting planned for days later at Skukuza game reserve between Mandela, de Klerk, Buthelezi and the King.

Okumu's request seemed absolutely impossible.

More prayer. The amazing Peter went to work that night with calls flying every which way.

And thus it was. Twenty-four hours later we again met Washington Okumu in Durban as he came, saw and conquered! And was then gone again.

A newspaper story on Thursday, 7 April said a plane carrying the presidents of Rwanda and Burundi had been shot down. No one began to guess where that would lead.

Next day was the Skukuza summit, which CBM and Colin Coleman had put so splendidly together. National hopes soared. Only to be dashed when it ended, deadlocked it seemed in doom and gloom. But the private good news from Skukuza was that Mandela and Buthelezi confirmed an invitation to Washington Okumu to come as official advisor to the international mediation exercise, now set for Tuesday, 12 April, just two weeks before the election. We were on a cliffhanger.

Rwanda exploded. News reached me next day that our African Enterprise team leader and his whole family had been tortured, lined up and shot. Other colleagues and friends were missing.

Would we go that way in South Africa?

Everyone knew we could. Rwanda and Bosnia remained daily on people's lips and the scenarios of those stricken places were haunting the minds of one and all.

'I Want South Africa on its Knees'

But prayer everywhere intensified. Additional impulse came from one extraordinary quarter. Many did not know what to make of it. Others, quite relaxed with the Bible's world view, were ready to listen. And believe. And obey.

A policeman in the Eastern Transvaal town of Nelspruit said he had seen an angel.

The word from the heavenly messenger was simple: 'I want South Africa on its knees.'

Colonel Johan Botha was transferred to Soweto, rather extraordinarily, on 16 June 1976, the day the township blew as thousands of black young people rioted in protest at Bantu Education and all its works. It was a day that shook the world. And South Africa was never the same.

Eight hundred people died.

Johan Botha had no part in that. But he was never the same either. God began working in his heart in new ways. He became a man of prayer and intercession.

But nothing had prepared him for the happening of 23 March 1994, just a month before the elections.

I talked with him about it.

'I share with great humility, awe and wonder what happened,' he said. 'It was just after 10.15 p.m. on the evening of 23 March. I had been reflecting on the events of the day and had been praying to Almighty God in all earnestness. Although I am Afrikaans-speaking, I find myself in countless situations these days where only English is spoken. For some unknown reason, I found myself praying in English, something that had never happened before. I had frequently been ending my prayers with the words: "Speak Lord, Your servant is listening." Thus, I was asking the Lord in all sincerity, "God, what is it that You want from us, what do You want from South Africa?"

'At that moment the whole extraordinary thing happened. An angel stood before me, bathed in a brilliant, indescribable light which hid his face, and answered, "I want South Africa on its knees in prayer." At that moment a light appeared with the word *gebedsdienskettings* (chains of prayer services) spelled out. I asked when we must do these things and the angel told me, "You have fourteen days. Go to the highest authority if it is necessary." "Would you then give us peace?" I asked, to which the angel responded, "You will experience the wonders of my workings."

Johan was overwhelmed and almost struck dumb with the awesome presence. And how could he convey any angelic message to the whole country? The notion was absurd. He would be laughed out of court. He bumbled out excuses, 'The people will not believe me, I don't have the courage. I shall cry if I have to recount what is happening to me now.'

While many might be tempted to dismiss such talk as outlandish or hallucinatory, I believed Johan, for he came through to me on the phone as a sane, calm and rational man of integrity. He went on: 'The angel replied, "What are a few tears compared to rivers of blood, my son?" He then put an arm lovingly around me,' related Johan, 'and I was even more overwhelmed and overcome.'

After the angel left, 'I lay and cried for hours. It was too much for me, too enormous, and it still is.' He got up, opened his Bible, and found himself in 1 Samuel 3 where Samuel got up three times after hearing a voice and went to Eli, the high priest, before being told to answer, 'Speak, Lord, Your servant is listening,' after which the Lord had appeared to Samuel. 'What greater certainty could I have wished for after that?' said Johan. 'I counted fourteen days from that moment. That meant 6 April, Founders' Day on the South African calendar.' The coincidence struck him as extraordinary. Johan told me the experience had turned his life 'inside out and upside down', even though he did have great difficulty at the time in coming to terms with his revelation. 'Not that I doubt what happened,' he said, 'but I wondered why it had happened to me. Was I sick, or having a nervous breakdown?' No. He was as fine and strong and normal as ever he had been. Instead came the simple realisation: 'I am privileged that such grace has been shown to me.'[2] He finally decided that he was 'prepared to go to any lengths to propound this message'. This included a conversation with President de Klerk who took his account seriously and encouraged him to call for more prayer, especially on Founders' Day.

As a result of Johan's courageous sharing of his amazing story, which the press also took seriously and picked up in a sensational way, thousands and thousands more people were moved to pray. Wednesday, 6 April 1994 was a prayer day called in response to this mysterious word. 'A miraculous success,' as Johan put it. Hundreds more churches, organisations and individuals around the country spent the day praying for peace and a breakthrough in the country's electoral crisis and national danger. 'In Nelspruit itself over eight hundred people of all denominations spent time at the amphitheatre where prayers began as the sun rose and the last service took place at dusk.'[3]

Other prayer rallies proliferated in the following weeks in such places as far afield as Rondebosch, Plettenburg Bay, Bloemfontein, Johannesburg and Pretoria, as well as in Botswana, Namibia, Ireland, Germany, the Netherlands and elsewhere in Europe.

Says Johan, 'The sixth April was a starting point in many major cities for hundreds of new prayer chains running right up to the election days.'

Divine Conditions

So whether the impulses to prayer came by means ordinary or extraordinary, nevertheless they came. And South Africa became in a very real sense a nation on its knees. And so one goes back and reflects yet again on God's words and promise: 'If my people who are called by my name humble themselves, and pray and seek my face and turn from their wicked ways, then I will hear from heaven and will forgive their sin and heal their land' (2 Chr. 7:14).

My own belief is that in that reality of national prayerfulness God's people met His special conditions in substantial measure and opened the way for a supernatural and miraculous moment of healing in the land as it came in April and May 1994.

Then Jesus . . .

Destiny waits in the hand of God, not in the hands of statesmen.

T.S. Eliot

The entry of the IFP to the elections was a diplomatic coup engineered by the Lord.

Musa Opiyo of Kenya

'What do you think can have happened, Peter? No sign of him.'

All passengers from the Kenya flight on the evening of Tuesday, 12 April had disembarked. And still no sign of Washington Okumu. And it was getting late. The reception at the Carlton Hotel for the international mediators had already been on the go since 6.30 p.m. It was now 7 p.m. We were going to be hopelessly late.

ANSWER TO BLOODSHED

All of a sudden, there in the airport, I felt deeply moved in my spirit. Words from Colossians 1:20, which earlier in the day had been ringing in my soul, came winging back – 'Making peace through his blood, shed on the Cross.' What seemed to come compellingly and overwhelmingly to me was that the Jesus Peace Rally, now so close at hand, was happening because of bloodshed. But the answer to this bloodshed was the blood shed by our Lord Jesus on the

Cross. It struck me that all the blood necessary for peace in South Africa had been shed on the Cross when we shed His blood and when He let His blood be shed by us. No other blood need be shed, for the incomparable Son of Man has shed all the blood necessary to save us from our sins and to make peace. Indeed, what can take away my sin? Nothing but the blood of Jesus.

Perhaps that was something to highlight at the rally. His forgiveness. And our need to forgive.

Yes, that was the message for the rally. It had suddenly come – in answer to prayer. In the middle of Jan Smuts Airport.

The Slow Suitcase

But now there were other things to think about. Okumu was missing. Then Peter had a brainwave, and correct it was, that he had been hijacked into the VIP lounge, where we later tracked him down, plus local South African body-guards now assigned him by Colin Coleman and CBM, the mediation organisers. No privacy now. High profile. And rightly so. His suitcase had been absurdly delayed, in fact it was the very last one off the aircraft, hence the inordinate wait. Extraordinary, especially for business class. In fact, mysterious. Anyway, we raced into town to the Carlton Hotel where it was all happening, and shot up to Okumu's room. 'I must change my suit,' he said. But with a rush of blood to the head, plus some cheek and a deep sense of urgency, I blurted out, 'Brother, you look great. Stay as you are. We must hurry.'

'You are right. Let's go.'

We were directed to an enormous room jammed with VIP guests and the world's media. Obviously the cocktail party part of the reception had ended and the press conference was winding up. Henry Kissinger was speaking at the end of it all on his hopes for the exercise. He said: 'We all have a very little time and usually in negotiation people adopt a position and then move three or four times until they come finally to their bottom line and best position. I would like to encourage all of you to start with your best position so that we do not have to waste time.' He then said he hoped it would all go well and sat down.

In the meantime, Okumu was ushered – past all the cameramen, film crews, photographers and journalists – to the top table where he was plonked down next to a startled Kissinger who gave him a huge hug. Master was greeting pupil.

To our delight, Okumu was asked to get up and say something. He stood and introduced himself, giving his full Kenyan name, and then said: 'I am very much humbled to be here and to make my remarks following my former teacher at Harvard, Dr Henry Kissinger. I am the Ambassador-at-large of the Forum for the Restoration of Democracy in Kenya and have been invited by the major parties to be the Advisor Extraordinary to the mediation process.' A couple of other remarks and he sat down.

Okumu had appeared like a bolt from the blue and numbers of folk seemed somewhat puzzled as to where he had come from. But he knew, and that was all that mattered.

Anyway, there now was this extraordinary giant, in more ways than one, recognised and established in the eyes of the media and the negotiators as Advisor to the process. If we had got there on time, he might either not have said anything at all, or else would have made remarks much earlier in the programme, in a general sequence of comments, and been less prominent. But in this situation he was the climax to the evening, the cherry on the top, as it were! Yes, perhaps it was indeed God playing His own card in a completely different and unorthodox way and showing sovereignty, even over delayed suitcases as He lifted His servant into the key position!

Okumu was seized upon by various media and interviewed. We slipped away thereafter from the gathering up to his room for dinner. He said Chief Buthelezi had taken him by the arm and warmly whispered in his ear: 'Since I first met you in 1972 I never knew that a time would come at a critical moment in my country's history when you would come to help us.'

As we reflected on the evening, and the late suitcase, Washington Okumu said it was always interesting to see how God works things out. 'You must never hit your head against a wall when the Lord works His delays. Good things always come from it.' Thus the man of faith.

'But,' he added, 'had I changed my suit beforehand and arrived five minutes later, I would have missed the whole thing.'

Hope and Despair

In the lobby after breakfast on Wednesday, while waiting for the professor and the negotiators to leave for their undisclosed destination, Dr Kissinger came into the lobby and Okumu graciously introduced me to him. When I said, 'How do you do, Dr Kissinger. Please know we will be praying for you to find solutions,' he looked at me quizzically.

Then he said, 'Thank you. I hope we *will* find solutions,' as he trundled away midst a crowd of VIPs.

We bade our fond farewell to Washington Okumu for the next few days, not expecting to see him until after the Jesus Peace Rally as he was due to be involved in the mediating exercise for conceivably as long as ten days. I remember thinking that things could only go up from there. We certainly couldn't go any lower.

'Leave Howick to me,' said Arthur Duncan to my colleague, Soh Chye Ann, still tirelessly at work on the Jesus Peace Rally. 'I'll take care of informing people in this town, hiring buses and getting people there.'

Colin le Foy and Josiah Dondo of the Assemblies of God in Durban spoke up in Norman Hudson's Jesus Peace Rally committee meeting: 'We've alerted all our churches and we'll be at King's Park in force.' All sorts of other pastors and church leaders said similar things.

Emmanuel Buthelezi toured townships pushing the rally. Zionist Archbishop Ntonga and Mbulelo Hina, of African Enterprise, went on Radio Zulu to promote the rally to its vast listening audience. Johnnie Frank, an Indian pastor from Chatsworth, was going all out. Cedric Coates and his Durban Task Force leaders weren't up one pole but up a thousand putting up posters everywhere! Lucy Carr and Jeremy Hovil painted 123 metres of banner for the stadium. Datnis Motors' huge billboard in Pietermaritzburg called out: 'Pray for the Jesus Peace Rally – Sunday 17 April.' Teams were roaming the length and breadth of KwaZulu-Natal in city and township, hamlet and village saying: 'Come to King's Park Stadium on Sunday 17 April.'

'But won't it be dangerous?' moaned the pessimists. 'What if horrendous violence and random shooting breaks out? Or planned assassinations?' No one wanted to dwell on such thoughts. And it didn't help that the New South Wales Rugby team, fearing explosions of violence, cancelled their match against Natal set for Saturday the 16th. In fact the fear factor of buses being fired on was very real, especially for people from the townships and from Northern KwaZulu-Natal. We knew numbers could be affected. Death threats to those planning to attend the rally were seemingly circulating in townships around Pietermaritzburg.

At the last minute several contingents from Ladysmith cancelled. One black pastor told us he'd had his whole congregation on their stomachs on the church floor, while AK47 bullets raked into the church through the windows during the previous Sunday's evening service.

Understandable as the fears were, a host of people pressed on with preparations for choirs, music, sound systems, platform, VIP invites, security, transport, publicity, finances and so on. Prayer intensified everywhere.

Zero hour was approaching. There were thirteen days left until the elections.

Later on Wednesday night, 13 April, Okumu called from Johannesburg to ask for special prayer. 'Please call our friends in England to alert the Lydia prayer groups all across the UK,' he said. He was going there and then into session with Kissinger and Carrington. He was thanking God that he seemed to have been granted favour with the mediators who were looking to him for counsel on many issues. But he was terribly frustrated about the hassle and deadlock now going on over seemingly new terms of reference inserted overnight on the election date issue, apparently by the government and the ANC and then presented to Inkatha. Seemingly neither the ANC nor the government was ready to countenance the notion of any delay on the election date: 27 April was non-negotiable.

Okumu's conclusion was that the situation was 'very grave'. There was an immense weight of responsibility now resting on him and all the mediators. He even asked me if we could get word to friends in England to see if Prime Minister John Major and President Bill Clinton could intervene directly with South Africa's senior political leaders. The word was passed.

Next day was for the professor one long, interminable and traumatic hassle, with the mediators doing all in their power and skills to keep the negotiations on track and save the exercise.

We put the Johannesburg mediation exercise, SOS-style, out on to the prayer chain around the country.

But by evening it was all over. The international mediation plan had aborted.

Said Kissinger to Okumu: 'I have never been on such a catastrophic mission and its failure now has cataclysmic consequences for South Africa.'

Just before I was to leave in the afternoon (Thursday, 14 April) to get away alone to a farm to prepare for the

Jesus Peace Rally, Okumu rang, distraught, to share the heart-rending news.

'Yes, the thing has collapsed. The mediation exercise is now over. The other mediators are appalled. Dr Kissinger has put his best shot at it and we are all reeling from shock. Everyone is going home in the morning and I will be on a plane to Nairobi tomorrow as well.'

I felt as if all the air had been knocked out of me and my spirit momentarily plummeted thousands of metres into an abyss of darkness.

'Brother,' I said, 'I see no way you can go. The Lord has not brought us this far only to let the whole thing fall apart now. Besides, you are in a very special way, I believe, God's man in this situation. Not that He has not used others. But you have a special role to play. Kissinger and Carrington may have to go, but not you. You need to soldier on alone. The Lord will help you and we will cover you constantly with prayer.'

'You think so?' said the big man reflectively.

'Yes, I think so.'

We prayed and rang off. I would head to my hideaway farm and we would keep in touch by phone with prayer needs. I felt very down.

At 5.40 pm. driving out to a farm in Balgowan, I clicked on my dictaphone and recorded: 'The news has just been formally announced that the international mediators are flying home tomorrow. I am sick at heart and devastated. As I see it now, all human answers, all human props, all the little human messiahs have fallen by the wayside and there now remains only the Lord and His intervention to keep our province and probably our nation together. The London *Sunday Times* last week rather crudely described the South African electoral process as "a bloody mess". That is pretty much what it has become.

'One trembles indeed for the whole situation unless the Lord intervenes, for matches and methane gas are now cheek by jowl thanks to a combination, I believe, of demonic activity and human folly. The Lord must deliver me now from feeling so sick at heart and enable me to turn my eyes upon Jesus and fulfil the ancient injunction of "Physician, heal thyself."'

I remember another thought coming to me very clearly on that drive. That night was to be the long-awaited Mandela-de Klerk TV debate. I had looked forward to it for weeks. There was a TV at the farm. I could watch it.

But the Spirit of God said: 'No. You've looked too much at man. Tonight, instead of watching more men, Turn Your Eyes Upon Jesus, and look full in His wonderful face.'

And I did. In front of an open fire. With my Bible. And alone.

Perspective began to return.

God could do it.

Late that night I left a message for Okumu at his Johannesburg Hotel: 'I am praying for you. Please do not give up.'

Carlton Hotel

The exhortation was hardly necessary, for the professor had not given up at all and was busy that night in no uncertain terms. Following press conferences held by Dr Kissinger on the one hand and Chief Minister Buthelezi on the other, the IFP negotiators met in gloom and despondency. Okumu had been invited to join them. Present at the meeting were Dr Willem Olivier, a Bloemfontein advocate who was constitutional advisor to the KwaZulu government, and Danie Joubert, Deputy Secretary General of the KwaZulu government. The two men approached Okumu afterwards and said they would like to meet with him that evening.

In addition Okumu spoke with Chief Buthelezi, who also felt the professor should stay on. Said the Chief later:

'Washington Okumu came up to me and we talked in a commiserating spirit about the thing going to pieces. He was very concerned about the consequences.'

In the evening, as planned, Okumu, Olivier and Joubert met and discussed things intensively until 2 a.m. when, if you please, they finally had dinner before working on for a further hour! They decided to contact Buthelezi early next morning in his hotel room to try and arrange for Okumu to see him.

Olivier's early morning call in the event drew a blank, for the Chief had apparently already left for Ulundi.

Lanseria Airport

Olivier phoned several airports, first Rand Airport, then Jan Smuts and finally Lanseria. Bravo! The Chief's plane was there! Olivier heaved a sigh of relief, which abruptly gave way to a moan of despair, as he learned that the Chief was already in his plane on the tarmac and ready to take off. But Olivier was not to be deterred. Under pressure from his pleading, the control tower officer radioed the pilot and asked him to request that the Chief return to the terminal building and wait for Okumu's arrival. The Chief agreed and the plane returned, the pilot considering it all highly irregular!

Olivier summoned a taxi and exhorted the driver, 'Please get Professor Okumu to Lanseria Airport quickly. Then bring him back here. This is very important. I'll pay.'

Buthelezi later recalled the events of the day. 'I went to Lanseria Airport to catch a flight to Ulundi. I had said goodbye to Washington Okumu the previous night. But at Lanseria a message was conveyed to me: "Professor Okumu wants to see you." I decided to wait for him a little while, which I did, but he didn't arrive. Two of my colleagues with me were going to the King's palace because there was a meeting scheduled that day between Archbishop Tutu and a delegation of clergymen who were going to see the King. So it worried me that we should not be late for the meeting with the King. So finally I said we should leave. I asked the manager to apologise to the professor and tell him that we had an appointment with the King.'

Okumu, meanwhile, was dashing by taxi to the airport.

'Driver, this meeting I have with Chief Minister Buthelezi is critically important. Please can you go a bit faster?'

The driver put his foot down. Okumu now sat paralysed as they began going through all the red lights without stopping.

'Driver, isn't this a bit dangerous?'

'Well, sir, we must get there. And if the police catch me, I'll tell them what you're doing, and they'll give us a full police escort.'

'Oh!' said Okumu, sitting back, resigned and holding on to his seat, 'Is that how it works here?'

The taxi driver looked in his rearview mirror a few minutes later.

The professor seemed lost in anguished thought.

Buthelezi picks up the story again. 'We were hardly airborne when the pilot said there was something wrong with the plane. The compass was playing up. And this was a brand new plane! So we had to return to Lanseria. Okumu by now was in the manager's office, having just arrived. I said to him, "You know, my brother, God has brought me back, like Jonah, because now there is something wrong with the plane, and it is obvious He wants us to meet."

'Washington Okumu then told me of a plan over which he had reflected very deeply during the night. He proposed to talk to Mr de Klerk, Mr Mandela and me to find out whether in fact we could still discuss how to make changes in such a way that I would be able to participate in the elections. The changes concerned the position of the King and the kingdom. Those were the main points. We talked at length and then decided to see each other on Sunday at the Royal Hotel in Durban on our way to the Jesus Peace Rally.'

The Lanseria conversation was momentous, 'in many ways a turning point,' said Okumu later.

The taxi now took the professor back to the hotel, its meter having run continuously throughout the encounter between the Chief and Okumu. The bill, Olivier was told, was R250. He looked startled. 'I do not normally carry much cash on me, but I had drawn money to give my wife for some shopping and other expenses. In my pocket was exactly R250! At that moment, I sensed that God was in this process and was working a miracle solution. I had a prayer group praying for me constantly and felt prayers were being answered.'

Okumu now took wings and began to pursue the plan, right, left and centre.

Later that Friday, he called Colin Coleman of the CBM who had given administrative back-up to the earlier international mediation effort. He asked Colin to meet with him at the Carlton Hotel to explain some exciting developments. At 10 p.m., Okumu briefed Colin and the two men discussed the matter. 'Coleman immediately saw the golden opportunity and suggested to Okumu that a meeting with Judge Krieglcr, the head of the Independent Electoral Commission, should be secured in order to determine in advance whether at this late stage the necessary ballot stickers could be printed to enable Inkatha to participate.'

Colin was thrilled at what was happening and, at Okumu's request, said he would do everything possible to assist him. He then agreed to set up a meeting with the IEC to discuss the logistics of including the IFP on the ballot papers and setting up voting stations in KwaZulu. Colin and the CBM now worked closely with Okumu in many of the efforts which followed.

Next day, Saturday, 16 April was a working day for lots of people. Olivier and Joubert spent the whole day with Danie Schutte at his home in Pretoria. Every possible solution was argued, analysed and reduced to detail. The documentation was so voluminous that when they went to a nearby restaurant for a working lunch, a private table normally seating twelve people had to be used for the three men and their papers!

Despite a very heavy election schedule, with the election only ten days away, President de Klerk was actually at his official residence in Pretoria. Danie Schutte phoned him to ask whether he would see the three men. The President agreed immediately and within minutes they met with him in Libertas. Straight and urgent talk followed for an hour. The three departed and further explored all of the options. They again saw the President at 7 p.m. After this meeting, Okumu spoke with Olivier, still at Danie Schutte's official residence, who reported to Okumu on the earlier discussions with President de Klerk in a one-hour phone conversation. A possible solution began to crystallise and suggestions were made for a possible draft of an agreement.

Meanwhile, Okumu had been meeting with Colin Coleman, Mike Spicer, Judge Johann Kriegler and IEC Commissioner Charles Nupen at the IEC Headquarters in Johannesburg. The daunting logistics of including the IFP on the ballot papers and setting up voting stations in KwaZulu were discussed. Judge Kriegler, to his great credit, immediately assented to the possibility of the IFP's last-minute entry. Colin Coleman emphasised that 'History should record that Judge Kriegler was extremely quick and bold in judging that this deal should be made possible. He was eager not to put logistics ahead of lives.'

*   *   *

Still later on Saturday, the professor met Colin Coleman again in Okumu's hotel room, where they drafted the first attempt at an agreement. Their task completed, they agreed that this agreement was watertight and departed excited by the knowledge that Okumu would take this text to Chief Minister Buthelezi next morning at the Jesus Peace Rally for an indication of acceptance. If this was obtained, Colin agreed to contact Mandela directly.

That Aeroplane

'Noel, what is the real story about Chief Buthelezi's plane?'

I was talking to Noel Potter, Managing Director of Osprey Aerospace in Johannesburg, whose pilots were on contract to the KwaZulu government.

'Well, I believe it was an act of God,' said Noel quite decisively. 'It was so inconceivable that our pilots, men of huge experience and capability, could have made an error so basic relating to the routine alignment on the ground of the plane's two compass systems. This is required to be performed while the aircraft is completely stationary. Conceivably in haste, they did this while the plane was being towed or not quite stationary. Although very unlikely, this could have resulted in the problem of one of the compasses acting up.'

I was a bit baffled and asked him to explain it all a bit more – which he did in detailed, technical terms, but simplified for a layman.

'The point is,' said Noel, 'that there was a unique sequence of events, each in itself unlikely, which could have occurred something like this: First, shortly after takeoff, a substantially incorrect compass reading was experienced, initially thought to be a technical problem with the compass system. Due to back-up systems, this is not a real problem on its own. Second, however, this problem initiated a sequence of compass and autopilot "snags" while airborne which, while not in any way dangerous or life-threatening, required the pilots to land the aircraft as a matter of precaution. Third, there was the unique timing of events so that a turnback to Lanseria, rather than a diversion to another airfield, was the logical action for the aircrew to take. The plane had been airborne for only eight minutes. So, had the problem manifested itself a few minutes later, the plane would have been rerouted to land at another airport and not at Lanseria where Professor Okumu was waiting.'

But now fasten your seat belt! The story is not over yet. Said Noel, 'When we performed the postflight check of the compass systems for the suspected technical problems, NONE WAS FOUND! The only conceivable explanation for the problem therefore was that the experienced and highly meticulous crew, through a very unlikely omission in the preflight compass alignment procedure, set in motion the extraordinary chain of events which ultimately resulted in Chief Minister Buthelezi's timely return to Lanseria. But it doesn't really add up.'

I asked Noel how the captaining pilot felt about it.

'Well, he was mystified, too,' replied Noel, 'and said as far as he was concerned it was "an act of God" especially when we later discovered what flowed from the subsequent conversation between Professor Okumu and the Chief Minister.'

Amazing, I thought, as we ended our conversation, this guy God keeps popping up all over the place.

No Disappointment

Back on the farm in Balgowan the phone was constantly on the go midst my struggling preparations for the Jesus Peace Rally. One called from the UK said media interest there was considerable. Next day my diary records that 'It was a fearful spiritual, emotional and intellectual battle to try and get it together', in spite of making it a fasting day.

Some verses from Psalm 22 particularly encouraged me:

'Yet thou art holy, enthroned on the praises of Israel. In thee our fathers trusted; they trusted, and thou didst deliver them. To thee they cried, and were saved; in thee they trusted, and were not disappointed' (vv. 3–5, RSV).

I asked the Lord that there be no disappointment in any way with the Jesus Peace Rally on Sunday.

JESUS PEACE RALLY

Sunday 17 April dawned bright and cheerful. It was good to think of a pre-recorded BBC interview going on right then calling a vast audience to pray for the rally and for the nation. Up in Newcastle in Northern Natal, Dr Guy Daynes went to early church. 'I was thinking of the Rally about to begin and about the plight our KwaZulu-Natal was in, when words, crystal clear words, came to me from the Lord: "I will intervene." I was amazed, not only by the message but also by the fact that He had given it to me. I told my wife excitedly about it there and then.'

As Carol and I reached King's Park Stadium, with ushers rushing everywhere with walkie-talkies as they guided cars and people in, one of the first people I saw was my colleague Peter who announced to me that 'We have lost Washington Okumu. I have been to the hotel where I was meant to find him, but can't locate him.' We both looked at each other quizzically knowing the professor is not one of those people who easily gets lost, whether metaphorically or literally! Clearly he was on some errand not known to us.

'What do you think of it?'

Okumu was at the Royal Hotel in Durban, holding out a handwritten document to Chief Buthelezi, also at this point en route to the Jesus Peace Rally.

The Chief looked at it, his eyes widening. 'I think this could work. If we could secure this with a last-minute sitting of Parliament before the elections to settle the matter of the King, then perhaps even now we could still come into the elections. Let me have it and we can talk about it at the rally to Danie Schutte and Jacob Zuma.'

The professor could scarcely contain himself.

At which point the phone rang. It was Colin Coleman who had managed to secure an appointment with Mandela. Colin wished to take Okumu to Cape Town there and then to see Mandela. An aeroplane had been organised by Colin through contacts with Anglo American. Colin and Mike Spicer were on board and would pick him up in Durban en route to Cape Town. Murray Hofmeyr of the CBM would meet them there. Okumu decided at once to skip the Jesus Peace Rally and go to meet Mandela. The Chief would press on to the stadium.

As the Chief arrived, several 'prayer ladies' gently took his arm and prayed for him. In fact prayer groups and prayer warriors had been in the stadium while others walked around it praying not only all day, but all the previous night as well.

Pressing on to the VIP lounge with Peter, I was thankful to see and chat with dear Jacob and Nkosazana Zuma, Queen Buhle and the Zulu Queen Mother, Danie Schutte and the press, some of whom were already interviewing Jacob.

But I must admit when I looked out over the 50,000 capacity stadium and saw it was not full, or going to be full, as I had hoped and dreamed, I felt disappointed because we were not going to be a jammed-out, full house. This seemed strange to me when the words seemed to have come so clearly the previous day at the farm that I would have 'no disappointment' with the rally and its outcome.

Anyway, as I headed to the briefing room behind the podium and walked from the 'players' tunnel', I looked back towards the main stand and was thrilled to see it filling up wonderfully. By the time the rally started, there was a huge throng with more and more people pouring in till we had about 25,000 or 30,000. But fear had taken its toll. One township which had ordered ten buses had had a wipe-out and all buses returned to base empty. Threats had carried the day in that spot and in many others.

But for the rest, it was joy, joy, joy all the way as singer Benjamin Dube from Soweto and his musicians got the thousands going with his high-powered Gospel songs setting feet dancing, bodies swaying and hands clapping. The most radiant sets of smiles you ever saw seemed to light up a myriad faces of South Africa's human kaleidoscope. Every race, colour, age, denomination and background was there. Journalists and cameramen from South Africa and around the world were also there.

My colleague Abiel Thipanyane stepped to the micro-phone: 'Will all those who have lost loved ones in the violence please stand. We want to pray very specially for you.' The whole stadium was suddenly pock-marked with hundreds of standing figures, heads bowed – men, women, teenagers, children, some quietly weeping already, a few convulsively, others just very quiet – overt emotions perhaps long since wrung out into a dull ache.

People gathered round them in little clusters, many of them in tears too, and prayed over them, often hands resting on head and shoulders, for comfort from 'the God of all comfort who comforts us in all our troubles, so that we can comfort those in any trouble with the comfort we ourselves have received from God' (2 Cor. 1:3–4). Yes, something like that was going on. One wondered what stories of horror and strickenness or heroism perhaps lay behind every person standing there in that noonday sun.

Reported the Natal *Daily News* next day with a banner headline: '30,000 say Yes to Peace', 'There were sol-emn and deeply moving moments, such as when people bereaved by political violence were asked to stand while others prayed for them.'

The Revs Cedric Coates, Reuben Timothy, Lukas

Meyer and Emmanuel Buthelezi led the throng in a litany of confession for our national, provincial and personal sins. Then the crowd was asked to form little clusters of five or six to pray together for peace and the situation in our war-torn province and to lift up our KwaZulu-Natal leaders and nation to God.

Now, as never before in our area, people recalled God's promises, especially the word to Joel which had come to mean so much to us:

Blow the trumpet [done] . . . declare a holy fast [done by many], call a sacred assembly [done]. Gather the people [done], consecrate the assembly [done], bring together the elders [done], gather the children [done] . . . Let the priests who minister before the Lord weep and say, 'Spare your people, O Lord' [just done] . . . Then the Lord will be jealous for his land and take pity on his people . . . [Was this about to be done?]

Yes, God had made His call. His people, representatively at least, had all across the province responded. And across the nation too, hundreds of individuals and groups were praying at the same time. And around the world – in USA, UK, Switzerland, Canada, Australia, the rest of Africa. And all who'd heard our prayer call on the BBC that morning.

And in that stadium, God's people were crying out to Him, as perhaps never before in our history.

'Lord, we have sought to do our part. Won't you now, supernaturally, overwhelmingly, overpoweringly, do Yours?'

Yes, only God could now heal KwaZulu-Natal and rescue South Africa. Everyone seemed to know that, and deeply. God's people had called. He would now hear, forgive, heal.

Up in the VIP lounge, while thousands and thousands

prayed, laboured and anguished before God, something else was happening.

Chief Buthelezi, with Okumu's handwritten document in his hand, showed it to Jacob Zuma, representing Nelson Mandela who had sent a warm greeting to the rally, but was now in Cape Town.

Zuma thought it could work.

A mighty moment was in the making. The Chief approached Danie Schutte, there representing President de Klerk who likewise had sent very strong assurances that he was with us and praying too.

Danie felt mounting excitement. A way through was emerging. There and then Danie called President de Klerk.

The beginning of a meeting of minds was under way on the road through for South Africa.

The Chief called an aide and said they must alert his plane. He would be leaving early for Ulundi where the Central Committee of the IFP would be gathering.

Okumu was en route to Cape Town with the CBM leaders for a 6 p.m. meeting with Mandela.

Thousands continued praying.

Here. There. Everywhere.

Reporters in King's Park Stadium were taking notes and getting their stories.

Next day the *Daily News* reporter would say: 'There were joyous moments when the crowd clapped, jigged and sang to the accompaniment of a gospel band, pleading to God to heal the land. Peace monitors and observers from overseas joined in.

'Messages of goodwill were received from, among others, State President F.W. de Klerk, Nelson Mandela, Zulu King Goodwill Zwelithini and KwaZulu Chief Minister Mangosuthu Buthelezi.

'Dr Buthelezi was also among a number of top local political figures who attended the rally.'

The *Daily News* story added: 'Methodist church leader Bishop Stanley Mogoba said: "We in this region are witnessing the worst human savagery this country has ever seen. We are a nation at war with itself. We fear the coming elections although we have waited for them all our lives."

'He said Jesus was the "general" that could turn a hopeless situation around.

'Mr Cassidy, in the main address, said: "We believe it can make a difference if many thousands of Christians will go out from this rally to every corner of KwaZulu-Natal freshly inspired as peacemakers and reconcilers."

'He welcomed last week's call for peace by the Zulu king. "The call is appropriate and timely. We are thankful and we urge all his followers to heed this call."'

The King had phoned the previous night, most anxious to be part of it all, and assuring us profoundly that he too was praying. 'Only God can see us through,' he had said, 'and God will not let us down. Above all I am praying for the political parties to listen to each other, understand each other's problems and do some compromising so the nation can be saved.'

He added: 'Tolerance and restrained language are the important things. And I want all my people together, from all the parties. You must say that from me, please.'

He had concluded the call saying: 'Without our Lord Jesus Christ we cannot achieve anything or go anywhere. Say that too.'

I had planned to, for sure.

He ended: 'I am with you in heart for the whole day.' That was encouraging.

To be sure it was 'a critical moment', as my own opening comments put it, in the history of KwaZulu-Natal with the world watching us and with a deep awareness in all of our hearts that we have effectively run out of human solutions. Our summits have failed, our international mediators have gone home shattered, our politicians are at their wits' end and it would seem almost impossible to pull off a free and fair election, particularly in KwaZulu-Natal. Indeed our provincial situation threatens to unravel and in doing so it could very adversely affect the whole process nationwide. This is a moment of human extremity. But man's extremity is also God's opportunity.

'In Scripture this is seen in many places in the two titanic little words: "**Then Jesus** . . ." Especially is this evident on the Cross when, after humans had done their lowest and worst *"Then Jesus* said, 'Father forgive them, for they know not what they do.'" In that word of forgiveness and in the power of the crucified and risen Christ stands the power we need in South Africa at this time.'

Among the calls made was another, very heavy on my heart and the hearts of all, I suspect, though seemingly impossible of realisation 'to the IFP even now at this zero hour, to enter the election even if they are unhappy with the election date. It will be in the long-term interests of all, including themselves, and it will make for peace.'

The rally was an extraordinary happening with the presence of God felt deeply and mysteriously. Archie Gumede, ANC stalwart and political leader in the old United Democratic Front days, was exhilarated: 'Ooooh! That was something really out of this world. I don't think anything like this has happened before in South Africa.'

As the service ended, people streamed out to cars, buses and trains. Khoza Mgojo, President of the South African Council of Churches and Umlazi pastor, turned to a friend on the platform: 'This is the turning point.'

Events moved fast now. Okumu and the CBM leaders in Cape Town met Mandela at six that evening. 'I was struggling with it all, almost wrestling,' the professor said later. In fact, by the time the 8 p.m. news came on television, which Mandela wanted to watch, I felt all was lost, and I had almost given up. But we got back to discussions. Suddenly, soon after 8.30 p.m., we seemed to have a breakthrough. Mandela offered his support, with certain conditions.'

Recalling the meeting later, Colin Coleman was 'extremely impressed with the agility of Mandela who, having just emerged from a rally where two people had died, was able to focus on highly sensitive negotiation. In no time, he saw its importance, identified issues to be clarified and had spoken to President de Klerk and Cyril Ramaphosa. The wheels were now turning.'

Danie Schutte later shared his end of things: 'After seeing Okumu's document at the rally I immediately phoned the President. I told him I had seen the document and it could be the beginning of something. Also that the document should then be discussed with Mandela and that Buthelezi was keen. The President was grateful. Roelf Meyer and I saw him that evening at Libertas in Pretoria. We had to move fast that night to get all the major players together in Pretoria next day, along with Okumu from Cape Town.'

Okumu, commenting afterwards, said, 'Danie was incredible. Amazing. All the way through the process, whenever I gave him anything for action or reflection, it was sent through to President de Klerk within minutes.'

IFP CENTRAL COMMITTEE MEETS

The Chief Minister later summarised his movements that late afternoon and evening.

'I participated in the first part of the Jesus Peace Rally but after discussing the document with Danie Schutte and

Jacob Zuma. I left to fly out for the meeting of the IFP Central Committee which we had called for that day. Then during the afternoon and evening I explained to them the terms of the Okumu document. We soon reached agreement that if these things were done in terms of the document of Professor Okumu, we would participate in the elections. We then formally passed a resolution to that effect.'

One IFP Central Committee observer said, 'When the Chief arrived he was beaming. He said, "I met Professor Okumu this morning and I have come from the Jesus Peace Rally. I have a document laying down the things we wanted in the agreement." I couldn't believe it. The Chief said he had phoned the King for his comments and he was in agreement. He wanted the Central Committee to discuss it quickly because they were expected to sign the document that evening in Pretoria. He read the document from Professor Okumu and asked for discussion. One by one the Committee stood up saying they were prepared to go into the elections on the 27th. There was no dissent. This was the mind of the Lord.'

One speaker then rose and said, 'God gave the vision that if we went to King's Park for the Jesus Peace Rally, He would give us a miracle.' At which the speaker, who had just come from King's Park, sat down, in tears and choked with emotion.

Plans for the proposed meeting of all the leaders in Pretoria next day, Monday, 18 April, went ahead full swing. 'In addition,' recollected Danie Schutte, 'we made a number of phone calls from the President's house, for example to Judge Kriegler, to find out possibilities on the ballot papers. This was my main concern: how could we in six working days before the election get the IFP on the ballot paper? But I was given the assurance, having been told for months that they would need weeks to have it reprinted, that it could in fact be done.'

Poor Judge Kriegler had a truly impossible task for his Independent Electoral Commission, already beleaguered in their work by a thousand no-go areas because of the violence. And now to adjust and get out 84 million ballot papers with six days to go! Surely the world's ultimate administrative nightmare.

THE STRONGHOLD PULLED DOWN

Back home in Hilton that night – and knowing nothing of the happenings in Cape Town, Pretoria or Ulundi at that very time, I was cast down. Profoundly so. It had been an amazing day. But preaching had been hard going with a late-running programme pressing and stressing me so that some key things seemed to have been left unsaid. I felt I'd failed.

Utterly played out, I sat disconsolate under my juniper tree like Jonah. But there was more than weariness and stress. There was a tremendous oppression and sense of darkness weighing over my spirit like a thousand black blankets of heaviness. I sat in my study and stared at the floor. I pleaded with God to forgive me for letting Him down. If only I could have seen three incredible encounters going on right then in three very different corners of South Africa.

Then says my journal, dictated late that night: 'I must record an astonishing thing which happened this evening, because about 9 p.m. I suddenly had a sense of a tremendous cloud, burden and oppression lifting. And as it did so, I seemed to hear the Spirit of the Lord within my soul saying: "The stronghold has broken and has been pulled down." I do not understand the full significance of that except that I believe something in the heavenlies has taken place and we can rejoice and be glad.'

I concluded: 'I feel absolutely smashed and wiped out as I turn in, but I know the Lord is in charge and everything can be left in His hands. We have done our part and He will do His.'

Little did I know.

I turned for bed, reflective. 'A stronghold has broken and been pulled down.' Before sleep I turned afresh to 2 Corinthians 10:3–6 and the Apostle's famous words: 'For though we live in the world we are not carrying on a worldly war: for the weapons of our warfare are not worldly but have divine power to destroy strongholds. We destroy arguments and every proud obstacle to the knowledge of God and take every thought captive to Christ.'

Yes, if a stronghold is an arena of individual or group thought not taken captive to Christ, and if by prayer a stronghold is broken and pulled down, then it means thoughts of great consequence were there and then being made 'captive to Christ'.

No, there would indeed be 'no disappointment' about the rally.

I believed. And went to sleep . . .

Meanwhile, the Anglo-American jet was racing through the night.

Coleman, Spicer and Hofmeyr were excited. They sensed breakthrough in the air!

Okumu, sitting behind them, was just plain weary and remained reflective.

'I left Cape Town,' recalled Okumu afterwards, 'on Sunday evening, 17 April, after nine. Mandela left at the same time going to East London. I arrived in Johannesburg at about 11.30. After midnight, I got Danie Schutte in Pretoria. He said a government car would fetch me about six in the morning. I then called Buthelezi and he told me he had shown my draft to Danie Schutte and Jacob Zuma during the Jesus Peace Rally when all the prayers were taking place. Chief Buthelezi told me that Jacob Zuma had no problems with the draft and that he himself would be in Pretoria for the scheduled meeting next day.'

Two Momentous Days

At the Union Buildings in Pretoria next morning, 18 April, the stage was set for two days of 'extraordinary meetings', as Richard Carter, personal assistant to President de Klerk, put it. Washington Okumu's special moment of destiny had arrived.

A plenary meeting of all those taking part met in the cabinet room under the chairmanship of President de Klerk, who welcomed everyone and, sensing the momentous nature of the occasion, asked for the meeting to be opened in prayer. He said he wanted each one present to have his full say.

Washington Okumu was called on first to address the developments that had occurred over the weekend and to explain his draft document. De Klerk then asked him to chair several meetings of the various party sub-groups where it was Okumu's task to help keep things on track. Observed Richard Carter, who was constantly alongside the President, 'Washington Okumu was that day clearly seized with the notion that he was doing something of extraordinary importance. His whole demeanour, intensity and even the sweat on his brow revealed a man utterly focused on the task at hand.'

Reflecting on the day, Okumu recalled that he and the President sat down at one point and looked at the draft document of proposals. 'He liked it and was very gracious. During the negotiations, I sat separately first with the Inkatha delegation who would then leave the room. Then with ANC's Cyril Ramaphosa, Joe Slovo and Mac Maharaj, whom Nelson Mandela had designated to negotiate with me until he could arrive the next day after his time in the Eastern Cape. So I would meet with each delegation separately in order, first of all, to ensure that we could allay their fears and, second, to find out what their respective problems were. And only when we thought we had a measure of success did we get the three delegations together again.'

That morning, across the city but in full view of the Union Buildings, Gavin Pryce Lewis and two other directors of Calcamite Sanitary Services were having a board meeting.

Midway through the meeting, and not knowing what was really going on over in Union Buildings, they suddenly sensed they should discontinue their meeting and focus their eyes on the Union Buildings and spend time in prayer. 'After praying,' wrote Gavin later, 'we were greatly encouraged and dared to believe that God had responded to our prayers.'

Prayers, unbeknown to the three board members across the city, were much needed.

They were also prevailing. For the whole day over in Union Buildings was one of steady progress, with both tough and gentle talk, as they all honed and fine-tuned the details of Okumu's document.

All knew a nation was at stake. At one point in the day, breakthrough seemed imminent. De Klerk, no longer grim but beaming, told the professor: 'I got on my knees last night and cried out to God to use this initiative of yours to save us.'

Observed F.W. de Klerk later: 'Okumu moved with instinctive and instantaneous understanding of what to say and do in relating to the major players.'

That night, recorded a CBM report published later, 'all the parties left the meeting upbeat'.

The process continued through the morning of Tuesday, 19 April.

Okumu reflected: 'Mandela, who had by now arrived, was very statesmanlike. He is a very amazing man. In fact in South Africa you have three amazing men of God in Mandela, de Klerk and Buthelezi. You people must appreciate them.'

The issue of recalling Parliament a couple of days before an election had seemed unthinkable, impossible and out of the question. The issue at hand, however, was the key issue of the Zulu King plus a few others. De Klerk said the impossible could be done. Minds must have boggled.

There were six days to go.

Knowing via a late-night call for prayer from Okumu that something, monumental was about to happen, I sat out the morning of Tuesday, 19 April at my office.

In the lunch hour SABC stopped its programmes to clear the way for a special announcement.

At last it came. De Klerk, Mandela and Buthelezi all spoke, the last ascribing the breakthrough to God. With six days to go, the Inkatha Freedom Party were entering the elections. Eighty million ballot papers would be adjusted. Parliament, unimaginably and without precedent, would be recalled to meet the day before the election.

South Africa's march into a democratic and non-racial future was back on track. Humans had come to the end of their tether. *Then Jesus . . .*

One person said: 'The moment it was announced I fell on my knees and praised God.'

Multitudes did the same. World wide.

I wept.

11 Election Day

The ballot is stronger than the bullet.

Abraham Lincoln

Free-ish and Fair-ish.

Weekly Mail headline

The general reaction to the sensational news from the Union Buildings on Tuesday, 19 April was euphoric. As the nation heaved the century's heaviest and deepest sigh of relief, the press reached beyond the ecstasies of relief to find a simple concept in which to frame the happening.

And 'miracle' was the word which emerged. Again and again it was there – often standing in simple and startling elegance at the head of articles or editorials. Throughout the secular press, the language of faith and God was in evidence.

Even *Time* magazine said: 'History has thrown up an authentic miracle.'

The *Financial Times* of London headlined its story 'God – and Realpolitik – Bring in Buthelezi'.

An article in the *Boston Sunday Globe* declared: 'Faith had role in Apartheid's end'.

The *Daily News* of Durban had a story: 'How God stepped in to save South Africa'.

The *Sunday Tribune* of Natal wrote: 'It's still the age of real life miracles, even if they take their time'.

Another paper felt beneath the surface and headlined: 'How the Miracle Happened'.

The *Johannesburg Star* wrote of 'The KwaZulu/Natal Miracle'.

The BBC's John Simpson had his view: 'It was the Jesus Peace Rally which tipped the scales'.

One South African journalist said: 'In our newsroom we have the toughest bunch of hardnosed what-nots, but in those days they were all rather shyly talking of God!'

Washington Okumu of course was swamped by the media, both local, pan-African and international. He did an amazing total of 136 radio and television interviews in only three days.

To one astonished reporter who asked him how it had all happened, he simply replied: 'It was God.'

To another he acknowledged: 'I feel humbled by this achievement, especially that we were able to reach it using the African option. But I believe in providential intervention and for that I thank God.'

Advocate Willem Olivier, who had played such a crucial role in negotiating the IFP's entry into the election, later told me that he realised that only intervention by God Himself could have prevented a disaster and even civil war, which might have resulted from the collapse of the international mediation process and secessionary thoughts among some others for KwaZulu.

'From, in particular, Thursday afternoon, 14 April, until the signing of the agreement at the Union Buildings the following Tuesday, the 19th,' Olivier said, 'I was aware of the Lord being in full control. Amidst my involvement in numerous consultations laying the table for the signing of the agreement, the reconvening of Parliament, amending the constitution in order to accommodate the King, and allowing the IFP on the ballot papers as a participant in the elections, I had constantly been aware that I was experiencing the unfolding of the Lord's answer to the many prayers of Christians.'

Businessman Terry Rosenberg expressed his feelings this way: 'I feel Washington Okumu's whole life and background had in some ways been a preparation for that particular week and for such a time as this.'

Everyone was in doxology mode. Praise lifted, as maybe never before in our nation, from a myriad souls.

Alison Hilliard of the BBC phoned us to do a one-hour interview. 'We see what has happened as a miracle and an answer to prayer. This programme will declare it as such to thirty-one million people.'

The IFP's Ziba Jiyane remarked: 'Having seen the resolution of this thing, those who still do not believe that God performs miracles are really fools! We were about to see our region enter the scourge of war which other brothers and sisters in other countries have seen. I don't say that lightly because I come from the decision-making centre in one of the key organisations here.

'You should be encouraged to know that in the ranks of many in the political groupings of both IFP and ANC, we politicians have become more keenly aware of the helplessness of humanity in our own wisdom. We had reached a point where, on our own, we had failed and were irrevocably fixated in the path of doom – until God's intervention.'

THE IMPOSSIBLE TACKLED

Although an extraordinary peace settled on the soil and soul of South Africa, nevertheless the task before the nation and especially before Judge Kriegler's Independent Electoral Commission was gargantuan. Their already impossible job had been compounded into the ludicrous. History had handed them the nightmarish assignment of not only adjusting eighty million ballot papers, but locating, manning and providing for about five hundred additional polling stations in KwaZulu-Natal within six days. With voting infrastructures being created at break-neck speed, there were inevitable problems.

Said IEC worker Tim Laithwaite from his corner of the electoral cabbage patch: 'When the IFP joined the process, there was pandemonium in the offices. Our co-ordinator nearly had a nervous breakdown. But by the grace of God, we somehow survived, with people working at least sixteen hours a day, trying to find suitable venues for stations and getting the police on board to organise security. In some areas, there was no infrastructure whatsoever.'

Then there was the scene that greeted one's eyes at the IEC headquarters in Durban in the days immediately prior to the election, which was enough to make anyone turn tail and run.

Businessman Terry Rosenberg was called upon to help out in KwaZulu-Natal at the last minute and gave a vivid account of the scene he encountered at the Durban headquarters:

'Calls were coming into one section from all over the region and the requests for provisions were being written down on little scraps of paper which were landing up on another floor of the building! When I went in, these important bits of paper were covering desks, falling out of drawers, a few were on the floor, and people even had stacks of them in their hands.

'They were so pushed for office space that some of the more enterprising IEC workers even set up shop in the lifts, going up and down all day! The main problem was that their cellular phones kept cutting out as the lifts ascended and descended.'

Thus the ups and downs of the IEC.

One young worker, Lucy Ntombela, said: 'I went to work there one day, but it was too much for me. I was so stressed out by the end of the day that I had to head home for aspirin and I didn't go back.'

Day of Democracy

But finally, at last, at last, at last, the day of democracy dawned as the sun came up over South Africa on Tuesday, 27 April 1994. The moment of liberation had arrived and the eyes of the world were watching as Africa began to claim back its final white colony.

As early as 2 a.m. people started heading towards polling stations in the moonlight, many wrapped in blankets to keep out the cold autumn night. The bomb blasts from the right wing's last desperate attempts to destroy the elections did not deter people, and by dawn there were many hundreds of queues snaking across the face of the country. The spirit of anarchy had been laid to rest and now people were waiting expectantly to have a say in their own future. An extraordinary feeling of optimism and hope penetrated the early morning cold and an almost tangible buzz of excitement pervaded every corner of the country.

As dawn began to break reports started flooding in, and the vision was overwhelmingly the same. It was of a new nation being born. This was the consummation of the miracle. The impossible was finally and actually happening. Blacks were being liberated from oppression and whites from guilt. And with the IFP in the elections, people could now go to the polls without fearing violent conflict there or even loss of life.

Determined to Vote

All across the land the stories were similar as people flooded towards polling stations, most for the first time in their lives. White farmers and black labourers arrived in trucks and queued together. Now there was no question of the 'baas' jumping the queue. An elderly woman in the East Rand was carried to a polling station in a wheelbarrow pushed by her son. Others walked from miles away, some hobbling painfully on crutches or leaning on walking sticks.

It soon became apparent that the process was riddled with the inevitable inefficiencies. Some stations did not open until well into the day. Some did not open at all on the first of what turned out to be three general voting days.

But it was the people on the ground who were the heroes of the day, people who defied the chaotic backdrop to the elections and, with rigid determination, refused to be daunted. On his way to vote, Thomas Mcira told a *Sunday Times* reporter: 'We are not worried that we will have to stand for hours before we have to vote. The sun can go down but we will wait. The time has finally come for us to be part of the country we were born in and for us it is a proud moment.' (*Sunday Times*, 1 May.)

One African lady, when asked by a reporter if she minded waiting for hours in the sun, replied: 'This is not a long time. I've been waiting three hundred and fifty years. I don't mind waiting a little longer.'

One Western Cape woman, eight and a half months' pregnant, was so excited about voting that it brought on her birth pangs. The baby was born a few hours later and christened 'Voter'!

The long wait did not prove worthwhile for one very ancient Afrikaner at a Cape Town polling booth. He told officials he wanted to vote for Field Marshall Jan Smuts (South African Prime Minister from 1939 to 1948)! 'Well actually, Sir, Mr Smuts died a little while back – 1950 I think?' At which the old man left in a huff, seemingly wondering how he'd missed that obituary notice.

At another station a woman of quite generous proportions was so delighted after marking her ballot that she took the paper and stuffed it deep into her bosom. She was taking it home, she said, to show her friends. History does not relate, but imagination can decide, whether there was a frantic flight of monitors or a spirited stampede to help solve the problem.

Identifying who first-time voters wanted to vote for was sometimes not so straightforward. One exceedingly short-sighted old gentleman said he wanted to vote 'for the one with the white hair', by which he meant Mandela. Only some very fancy footwork by a monitor prevented his vote going to right-wing Freedom Front leader General Constand Viljoen, whose snowy hilltop is even whiter than Mandela's, and whose picture, along with other party leaders, was on the ballot paper.

Illiteracy, which in some areas ran as high as 80 per cent, was sometimes dealt with as the voter would say 'Nelson', or 'Mandela', or 'Gatsha'. One voter on the verbal option flummoxed the monitor by announcing the name 'Harry' rather grandly as if introducing himself. The monitor was about to say, 'Hello Harry, my name's Tim,' when he realised the voter was giving his vote to Harry, you know, Harry Gwala, KwaZulu-Natal Midlands' leader of ANC.

'Oh yes – Harry,' stammered the monitor. 'Just put your cross there, please. Next to Nelson. Thank you.'

And of course standing in queues, which often snaked away round street corners or hillsides literally for several kilometres, was exhausting for many. At one booth some resourceful ladies discovered that if you had a baby in your arms you would often be moved up to the head of the queue by thoughtful officials. One baby, on heavy duty, was passed surreptitiously from 'mother' to 'mother' and managed to promote twelve so-called mothers to the head of the queue. Top marks to motherhood!

More seriously, the overwhelming and moving picture was of polls bringing South Africans together at last. Most astonishing was to see Inkatha and ANC supporters, sworn enemies and bent on killing one another just a week previously, now standing peacefully together in queues, laughing, chatting and ribbing each other in general bonhomie and apparent reconciliation.

'Who would have thought that in places like Umlazi, ANC and IFP voters would queue happily together,' said SACC President Khoza Mgojo. 'It was quite unbelievable and a miracle from the Lord.'

And then there were 'maids and madams', standing side by side, united in their long wait. On Johannesburg's Radio 702, a man later told how he had queued for four hours with his maid. 'We got to know each other better in that time than we had in ten years living under the same roof.'

Everywhere the atmosphere was one of tolerance as hundreds of little miracles were occurring across the country in what was, collectively, a totally new experience. People showed, through their patience, that they were tired of violence and were now united in their commitment to the dawning of democracy and a new day in South Africa.

'DAY OF OUR LIBERATION'

Before going to cast his vote, Nelson Mandela went and laid a wreath on the tombstone of the ANC's founding president, John Dube. Appropriately the inscription on the tombstone read: 'Out of the darkness into the glorious light', which was taking on a new poignancy. After casting his vote at a Durban school, Mandela came out with a message true to the spirit of what had occurred in South Africa: 'We are moving from an era of resistance, division, oppression, turmoil and conflict and starting a new era of hope, reconciliation and nation-building.' The man who had spent so much of his life working for this moment, called it 'the day of our liberation'.

Interesting voters who turned up at a polling station in Soweto's Orlando West were Pik Botha and Roelf Meyer who were received with no apparent ill feeling when they arrived in Soweto of all places to cast their vote!

In Cape Town, Archbishop Desmond Tutu was so

overjoyed as he cast his vote that he was moved to dance a rather unAnglican jig! 'Today is a great day for all our people, and I mean all our people, black and white,' he told a waiting crowd. He compared voting for the first time with falling in love!

IEC

One cloud which constantly threatened to overshadow the whole process came from the organisational problems of the Independent Electoral Commission. Allegations of irregularities were flying across the country and words such as 'sabotage' were being thrown in the face of the IEC slogan calling for 'substantially free and fair elections'. But anyone who saw the sweat and long hours under intense pressure that IEC workers put in to enable the election to happen would have restrained their criticism.

The IEC was thrown out of gear in many places because South Africans emerged to vote in such unexpected numbers. The census figures turned out to be wildly inaccurate in some places, as the hidden faces from apartheid's oppression began to appear. A remarkable illustration of this was in the Orange Free State where 115 per cent of eligible voters – 200,000 more than expected – turned out!

Ballot papers were soon running out. Where some of the eighty million ballot papers ever got to one will never really know. One person in the Cape phoned a friend of mine and said: 'What on earth should I do? I have just had 100,000 blank ballot papers thrown over the fence into my backyard.'

At other times polling stations ran out and monitors phoned the IEC for more. Because of transport problems, bundles of ballot papers were in desperation handed out to taxi drivers to deliver to station X or Y. Any politically dedicated taxi driver could of course have had a field day and no doubt some did. Then again,

Jane Stuart, an IEC worker in Johannesburg, saw the desperate situation this way: 'Towards the end of the election period, ballot papers were being sent out in taxis since no transport was available. For the purist, this was of course unforgivable. But the objective was to enable people to vote and, practically, it would have been nigh on impossible for any subversive force to figure out what was going on, let alone try to subvert it. My opinion is that those taxi drivers played their parts very ably in allowing the new South Africa to be born.'

Some ballot bundles were even found tossed into fields. Some said this was sabotage by white right wingers who'd got in on the IEC system. Who knows?

Then there was the bundle of ballot papers, all neatly wrapped, which came in with 60 per cent checked ANC, 30 per cent IFP and 10 per cent NP. Some wiseguy had obviously studied the pre-election polls for his area!

Not surprisingly people began to outnumber available ballot papers, massively so in some places. In KwaZulu-Natal the situation became fraught. Terry Rosenberg was again one of the people contacted by frantic IEC commissioners at 6 p.m. on Wednesday, 27 April, the first of what turned out to be three days of general voting. They asked if he could help out by printing six million additional ballot papers overnight. They were needed by dawn the next day!

'We managed to get hold of our company's printers and Max Nathan, the key person there. When we mentioned on the phone to Max what we needed, he went very quiet,' said Terry.

Not surprising, I'd say. The guy had probably fallen to the ground unconscious.

'Anyway,' Terry went on, 'with the help of Stan Jabour, we mobilised the printing industry virtually within minutes and set about the task. We had teams controlling the forms, observers watching to check that all was legally sound and teams to arrange them in piles according to where they needed to go. Another team then loaded them on to trucks and sent them off to an airport where others were allocated to travel with the forms for security reasons.

'Then,' he went on, 'we had another logistics team in place seconded to us by the South African Air Force. Their job was to prioritise the needs and work out an appropriate transportation plan to get the ballots to where they were most urgently needed and later to the centres which were better provisioned. We had three different types of chopper and small planes which all had different capacities so we had to work out the weight of the forms and load them accordingly. Then we had another team figuring out who would be on the receiving end and how we would control that. So all these teams were working simultaneously and I was trying to co-ordinate the whole thing. But the South African Air Force was great.'

Voting would go on officially till 8 p.m. then start at 6 a.m. next morning. No time to lose if things were to be salvaged.

For me 27 April, once I'd voted, was spent trying to get my much neglected desk in hand. Mid-morning, Danie Schutte dropped in, bodyguards and all, and said, 'I just wanted to come by and say that, for me, the miracle began when I met Washington Okumu in this lounge a few weeks ago. You see, all the formal processes had aborted. God had to use the informal. We had done everything humans could do, power politics, money and all. Thereafter the Lord Himself had to rescue us.'

Just before supper my secretary, Colleen Smith, rang urgently.

'You must watch the 8 o'clock news. Things are looking a bit heavy out in Ulundi. The Chief says there are so many problems and so much skulduggery they may pull out of the elections.'

I was appalled. No one could afford for things to go wrong now when the country had got this far.

I waited anxiously for the 8 o'clock news. To my great alarm there was Chief Buthelezi, obviously tense, describing extensive administrative failures and break-downs in the polling procedures, some rural locations without polling stations, others where the ballot papers did not arrive, or others where seemingly the ballot papers arrived but the IFP sticker was not affixed, and so on, or else electricity-driven ultraviolet lights arrived for places where there was no electricity. Sadly this story, he said, was being repeated in quite a few other places throughout the country, so that there was a 30 per cent non-success rate in even the Reef and PWV areas. In most other parts of the country there were apparently significant failure rates as well. The hint was there that the IFP would have a Central Committee meeting that very night and possibly pull out of the election.

I phoned Danie Schutte at once. He indicated that he too had seen the news and was very concerned. He was just phoning President de Klerk and Judge Kriegler. He said he might go out to Ulundi that night.

'I think you should,' I replied, 'and I'll come with you to give some prayer backing.'

The Lord's wisdom would be needed by all. Otherwise decisions could be taken in the flesh, or in human impetu-osity or through wrong counsel. And then what?

Danie was in accord. The fruits of Kolobe, perhaps. 'Meet me at Oribi Airport in an hour. We have a military jet coming from Waterkloof Air Force base. Advocate Moseneke, Vice-Chairman of the IEC, will fly up from Durban.'

I changed and packed a small bag – in case an overnight stop were required.

'What are you doing? Where are you off to now?' said Carol with that look reserved for delinquent husbands. 'You're still sick, you know.' This remark followed my having been consigned by my doctor to bed for four days because of chronic exhaustion.

'Sweetheart, I'm flying to Ulundi.'

'Now?'

'Yes, now!'

Incredulity. 'You're not just sick, you're also insane!'

Anyway, Carol, amazing and astonishing lady that she is, quickly saw the importance of the errand and the peril to the election if at this stage the IFP withdrew. She began phoning intercessors to back it all up, including Derryn Hurry, who alerted those at the prayer vigil, still going full-force day and night at the Anglican Cathedral in Pietermaritzburg.

In the car on the way to the airport I sensed we needed to go claiming the Psalmist's word that 'Power belongs to God' and Jesus's word, 'All power in heaven and earth belongs to me.' One could see how Old Screwtape might throw the ultimate political spanner in the works and have some impetuous decision made that night which would have put the entire process into convulsion and catastrophe.

Arriving at the airport, I found no one. Just a couple of lone air traffic controllers in the tower. The friendly fellows served me a cup of tea up in the tower and we waited.

Suddenly down there in the dark a limousine pulled up. Several shadowy figures stepped quickly through the gates and out on to the landing strip.

It was Danie, plus his media assistant and a private secretary. No sign of the plane. Danie's portable phone, the final symbol of the space age, was not working. So we waited.

Then to our relief, the silence of the night was suddenly broken by the sound of the jet which, with blinking lights, now raced in on to the runway. It was 10.15 p.m.

Back in Durban, while Advocate Dikgang Moseneke

caught his plane to Ulundi, Terry Rosenberg was having yet more problems with his all-night marathon.

Remembering the hard day's night, Terry related: 'About 9.45 p.m. I had another call from Charles Nupen, one of the dedicated electoral commissioners, telling me they had run out of invisible ink.'

This ink was used in the polling stations to stamp the back of voters' hands. The stamp would then become visible under an ultraviolet lamp, which prevented people from voting more than once.

'The manufacture of the ink was not a problem but, in order to get the 4,000 one-litre containers to hold it, we had to call one of the directors of Barlow's out of a dinner party in Johannesburg and then commandeer a plane to get the bottles to a mass of different locations.

'Then, unbelievably, a call came through a little over an hour later to say that the IEC had now run out of ultraviolet lamps!

'Of course the forms are no use,' continued Terry, 'unless you have the ink. And the ink is no use without the ultraviolet lamps because you can't then check to see if someone has voted.

'That blew our minds and we didn't know what to do. So I went into the operations' room, stood on a table in front of about sixty people, and asked if anyone had any ideas! Finally a Jamaican lady remembered that Lesotho had used these lamps in their recent election.

'So we looked up the appropriate minister in the international directory, woke him up in the dead of night, and told him about our crisis. He put us in touch with Lesotho's electoral officer whom we also awakened!'

Astonishingly, midst his drowsiness, or perhaps because of it, he agreed to supply the extra lamps.

The only problem was that Maseru Airport didn't open until 7 a.m!

'Oh dear,' moaned Terry. 'Get me some coffee.'

*　　*　　*

Back at Oribi Airport our party settled back into the Cessna Citation jet which pushed one's front against one's back as it plunged forward with massive acceleration and rose into the night.

In twenty-five minutes we were in Ulundi and by 11 p.m. were with Chief Buthelezi and his senior electoral advisers and top colleagues in the same conference room where a few weeks previously, with Washington Okumu, we had met the IFP leadership.

A cluster of ten or twelve others were there and the Chief looked absolutely cross-eyed with exhaustion. We immediately got down to business, disappointingly without an opening prayer, but I was doing plenty of secret praying, make no mistake!

An extraordinary list of election irregularities, mishaps and organisational disasters was presented. It seemed to go on *ad infinitum*. There were situations where people turned up to find no polling station, or else there was a polling station but some of the equipment was missing, like the ultraviolet lamps or the invisible ink, or even the ballot boxes themselves. In a couple of cases the electoral officials themselves were missing!

Sometimes people went through the electoral procedure, having their hands stamped with invisible ink, only thereafter to find there were no ballot papers at the end of the line, or that they could not vote for some other reason. One could well imagine the fury of such people, now marked as having voted, yet they had not voted! Nor would they be able to vote, for the fatal liquid stamp was upon them.

Then there were cases where polling stations could only handle 3,000 people in the day but more than 10,000 turned up. Some then had to leave, often furious, having waited a whole day without voting.

We were then told that in places as far afield as Maputo, London, Durban, Pietermaritzburg, and all over Northern KwaZulu-Natal, there were cases of ballot papers without the IFP sticker. One could understand the Chief Minister and other folk feeling upset and deeply concerned.

One might have been tempted to feel some of these were put-up stories. But all the reports seemed to have the ring of truth and authenticity and were accompanied by photostat copies of letter after letter from different parts of KwaZulu-Natal, and often from around the country, all speaking about this kind of electoral procedure mess up. Undoubtedly thousands of people had been affected. There was indeed a problem, but Danie and Advocate Moseneke were terrific. Indeed, Danie's calls there and then to Pretoria got planes flying plus some sixty extra personnel, ballot boxes, ballot papers, ink and ultraviolet lamps from Pretoria ready to be on-site by dawn. Moseneke also promised to move heaven and earth with IEC machinery.

My little 'ha'penny-worth' of input stressed that, in a first-time election like this, we all needed to be realistic and content with a seven out of ten score, which the Chief Minister indicated would satisfy the IFP. No point in expecting perfection. Second, the election in South Africa could not afford to go wrong now and had to be saved. Anything that was necessary to secure a solution should be secured. Third, my question to the Chief Minister was whether he felt a day extra would make a difference. He said 'perhaps', but wondered if one day would be enough. My urging, for what it was worth, to Advocate Moseneke and Danie Schutte, therefore, was to explore the allowance of an extra day for voting in all areas requiring it.

Danie and Moseneke said this was a complicated process involving a tripartite agreement between the TEC, IEC and the State President. Clearly it was evident that this could not be decided in the next few hours. My plea then to the IFP leadership was to accept the dilemma that Moseneke and Danie were in and the bona fides of Advocate Moseneke's pledge to fix things. They, for their part, should be content with a list of places where there were genuine problems justifying a prolongation. This could be granted within the terms of reference of the IEC and Danie and Advocate Moseneke recognised this.

I was privileged to be able to close the exercise in prayer for the Lord's hand on it all. I reminded them of 1 John 3:20: 'God is greater.'

It was well after 2 a.m. when we were airborne again. The welcome embrace of blankets and bed finally came after 4 a.m.

'We can't land at Maseru Airport before 7.00 a.m.,' moaned Terry Rosenberg to his late-night extras slaving on the extra ballot papers, ink, and ultraviolet lamps.

'No alternative. Our planes must fly and be hovering over that airport at 6.45. Then they can drop down at 7.00 and do the job.'

So the Dakotas got there early, circled for fifteen minutes, then swooped in to pick up the 1,500 ultraviolet lamps in a frenzied flurry, and then speed back to Durban to transfer them in minutes to planes flying to every part of KwaZulu-Natal.

'So now,' said Terry, 'we had forms going out in one set of planes, bottles coming in on another and lamps being transported to different locations in yet another. Anyway, it all somehow came together, mainly due to the hard work and dedication of many, many dedicated people – lawyers, accountants, salespeople – all genuine South Africans happily donating their time to the country they loved. Two of the most impressive people in all the turmoil were commissioners Charles Nupen and Dikgang Moseneke.'

As the Province woke up next day, the election was back on track.

Meanwhile – Back on the Ground

Meanwhile back on the ground, IEC officials and election observers were profoundly grateful when the materials did begin to arrive. Things had got very tense in some areas and hair-raising stories were beginning to seep through to IEC headquarters. One official returned to his polling station empty handed after going in search of ballot papers. Someone in the 3,000-strong queue found a rope, and before the poor official knew what was happening he was hanging upside down from a tree! A police patrol soon came by and let him down. History does not relate what then happened at that station. A hung vote, perhaps.

Added one election observer more seriously: 'If the IFP had pulled out midway through, a mass of IEC officials out in KwaZulu-Natal would have been killed.'

The other problem was that, in the IFP strongholds, voter education had been made impossible. Only two weeks previously, on 11 April, seven people distributing leaflets urging people to vote for 'a better South Africa' were hacked to death. This meant that many of the voters in KwaZulu-Natal, a high proportion of whom were illiterate to start with, had no idea what was going on. Many were bewildered by what was a very complicated voting process and ballot paper. Some were quite paralysed, seeing twenty-six or so names, flags, photos, etc.

But among the chaos and confusion people were determined to do their bit to see the final extinction of apartheid. Nothing could stop democracy now and the ultimate focus of the picture was not on the shortcomings and eccentricities of the over-pressurised voting mechanisms, but rather on the human spirit winning through. Barefoot or richly clad, they shuffled forward in the queues and waited their turn, each one adding a touch of colour to the rich mosaic of South Africa.

Redundant Security

All the eccentricities and oddities apart, the electoral show thus went on. And before the amazed eyes of the television-watching world, the elections unfolded peacefully.

It was the mark of a new day in Table Mountain near Pietermaritzburg, the site of some of South Africa's most appalling violence. Election observers, the ones who had been brave enough to go there, witnessed an almost unbelievable atmosphere of calm. An extraordinary mood of peaceful determination and patience had taken hold in an area previously ravaged by massacres.

In Alexandra township, not a single violent crime was reported, where before an average of twenty murders a week and a hijacking every twenty minutes had made the township something close to a war zone.

Likewise in Pietermaritzburg, notorious for its high crime rate, not a single episode was reported of any kind of crime over the four days of the election.

How different from the predictions. The largest security operation in the history of South Africa had been set up to deal with the expected violence. About 100,000 police were deployed and there had been the largest call-up of army reservists in history. Most felt redundant as they stood watching the patient optimism of the peaceful queues trailing into polling stations.

So what of all the predictions of war? South African Police Commissioner General Johan van der Merwe described the almost complete lack of violence during the election process as a victory for peace. He told the *City Press* newspaper: 'This is nothing short of miraculous and provides the basis on which to extend further the spirit of reconciliation so desperately needed in South Africa.'

Hundreds of overseas journalists who had come for a ringside seat at the opening bout of Planet Earth's new civil war left for home, almost disappointed. Kayode Soyinka, London editor of *Newswatch*, a Nigerian publication, came out expecting the worst and headlined his election story: 'The Civil War that never was'.

As Duncan Buchanan, Bishop of Johannesburg, put

it: 'That particular week in the life of the country was probably the most peaceful we've had in the last forty or fifty years. Only God could have organised a scenario so wonderfully peaceful.'

Tainted with Sadness

Yet there was a constant awareness that the peace of the election came out of a violent past soaked in blood. There were many empty spaces in those queues from people who had died for precisely this. It added a dignified sadness to the elation and euphoria. Voters could only be haunted by memories of Sharpeville and Soweto, Bisho and Boipatong and scores of other tragedy spots etched in the nation's memory. Decades of injustice and oppression could not be wiped from the memory just by putting a cross on a piece of paper. On South African television, a dignified elderly man in the Transkei voiced this feeling: 'If only the dead could have risen from their graves to witness the fruits of their struggles . . .'

Elizabeth Ntho, ninety-three years old, had her right leg blown off in the 1960 Sharpeville massacre. For the first time since that terrible day, she visited the graves of the sixty-nine friends who had died. It was for her a day of liberation tinged with sadness and grief. As she commented to a BBC reporter: 'I'm so old there's nothing left in me, but I'm so proud because my children will live in freedom.'

Free-ish and Fair-ish

Was it free and fair? If there are relative degrees of freeness and fairness then South Africa, which seems to be in the business of the extraordinary, seemed to achieve such a thing. The election was certainly riddled with unconventionality. One election observer posted in the heart of KwaZulu-Natal told how she had spent her time watching an Inkatha supporter openly intimidating voters inside one polling station. When she asked the presiding officer to have him removed she was told it was impossible because he had issued death threats to all the IEC officials if he was not allowed to stay. One look at the collection of 'cultural' and not-so-cultural weapons outside the door was enough to silence any well-meaning official. This has no doubt happened in several situations.

Supporters of other parties did similar things. Noted one Imbali resident: 'Sure, the ANC cheated. The IFP cheated. Yes, I think it was free and fair!' Undoubtedly some white right-wingers, perhaps trained in the dirty tricks brigade of yesteryear, were also very busy through those days doing all they could to subvert.

But South Africa's first non-racial democratic election staggered through, warts and all, and into the final counting process.

'Free-ish and Fair-ish' was the headline in the *Weekly Mail*.

FINAL COUNTING

At times the counting of votes seemed, if anything, to be even more hazardous than the voting process itself. Some ballot boxes were disappearing into thin air, while others seemed mysteriously to appear from nowhere. Many were found unsealed and the whole process of reconciling ballot papers was very soon scrapped. By 4 May, the *Natal Witness* reported that, so far, spoilt papers were running fourth with more voters than the CP and PAC put together!

In one counting station, about 200 extra people arrived to help out, no doubt having heard there was good pay to be had as 'counters'. They were all waiting outside the gate when it started to rain. The beleagured IEC officer in charge took pity on them and let them come into the counting station. He already had 200 people in a room built for 150 and now, with the extra 200 people, whom in fact he did not need, there was pandemonium. In the end he stood up on a table and said, 'Those who are inside are definitely accredited and able to be counters. And others outside are also getting wet. Please could you alleviate the pressure by going outside.' He then had a situation where the people inside (not needed) should have been outside and the people outside (definitely needed) should have been inside, while he himself probably wanted to be neither outside nor inside but a hundred miles away at home! Fortunately the police arrived and, midst all the toyi-toying, were eventually able to sort things out.

In Johannesburg and the PWV area, the wheels threatened to come off altogether until the IEC called upon Methodist Bishop Peter Storey and Anglican Bishop Duncan Buchanan to help out. They immediately set up an all-night telephone chain to contact church leaders and clergy and eventually had 1,200 people assembled by dawn outside the Rhema Church complex, all of them ready to be trained and accredited.

With a list of 720 counting stations they then deployed people around not only the PWV area but also arranged for some to be flown to other regions around the country.

As Buchanan said later: 'The end result was that God achieved a remarkable thing. In almost every counting station there was a Christian presence of people doing something important for the Lord. And in the process God honoured that in the most remarkable and wonderful way.'

But to look at the smaller cameos and the local pictures is to miss the bigger point. Even before the results were announced there was an atmosphere of jubilation and victory throughout the country. The election was about liberation as much as it was about democracy. There were no losers except apartheid and the main evidence of that was the fact that no one had died in political violence in what surely must rank as the most peaceful four-day revolution the world has ever seen.

In his speech conceding defeat, President de Klerk said in an utterance surely without political precedent for a losing campaigner, 'God has been very good to us.'

A MIRACLE OF GOD

And, regardless of political affiliation, everybody agreed this had to be some sort of miracle. As Michael Buerk said when he ended the BBC news on the evening of 26 April, 'It's not the results but the fact that it's happening at all that is making history.'

Former Zambian President Kenneth Kaunda, serving as an election observer, said: 'I would say without hesitation, it is a miracle, a tremendous start to a new beginning.'

Even the hard nuts in the media were incredulous about what they were seeing before their very eyes. As John Humphrys wrote in London's *Independent* on Sunday, 8 May 1994: 'Better, it seems, to boil babies for breakfast than for a hack to admit that something akin to a miracle has happened in South Africa.'

In the UK's *Daily Mail*, a report read: 'What has happened in that beautiful, tortured land is a political miracle . . . Today is for celebration, for optimism and, yes, for faith. The whole world unites in offering its blessings and good wishes to our newest and most remarkable democracy.' (28 April.)

Khoza Mgojo of SACC emphasised: 'It was more than a miracle. I don't know what to call it. But what happened in the election was for sure a miracle from the Lord. I personally believe the breakthrough came in the prayer meeting at King's Park Stadium. The people of God came together and cried and the Lord listened. That for me was the turning point in the elections.'

The emotion of the moment was eloquently described by Mondli waka Makhanya in the *Weekly Mail and*

Guardian (29 April – 5 May): 'I made my cross next to the picture of Nelson Mandela, a man who just a few years ago I could only sing about and whose photographs I used to hide at the bottom of the family deep freeze. As I put my ballots in the boxes I almost suffocated with emotion as I realised the sanctity of the act I was performing . . . This was the end of a nightmare.' He later added: 'I recalled the emotions of the previous night, when I watched the death of the flag that symbolised all that was cruel and evil to me. In the privacy of the car, under cover of night, I wept.'

An old man in the PAC section of Soweto summed it up: 'God is with us today. This is what He wants for us.' (*City Press*, 1 May.)

Bishop Eric Pike of Port Elizabeth, who could have been speaking for multitudes, wrote in his pastoral letter: 'I hear people who are not even churchgoers, indeed some who may not even claim to be Christian, acknowledging quite openly that our peaceful transition to democracy has been a "miracle", a work of God's grace.'

I too believe that. With all my heart.

And because I do I have sought, in the manner of Isaiah, to 'write it . . . in a book, that it may be for the time to come as *a witness forever*' (30:8).

And, with the Apostle John, I must also acknowledge, of course, that 'there are many other things which are not written in this book . . . but these are written that you may believe – that Jesus is the Christ, the Son of the Living God – and that believing you may have life in His Name' (20:30, 31).

Epilogue

THE FUTURE

12 How Then Should We Live?

The breakthrough in South Africa is the most significant thing which has happened in Africa this century.

Former UK Ambassador William Peters

In the year that King Uzziah died, I saw the Lord.

Isaiah 6:1

What does a nation do when it has lived through a miracle, when it has seen the Living God intervene on its behalf and bare His arm in answer to prayer? How then should it live? How bear the divine destiny which has devolved upon it?

Can such a nation go on with business as usual? Dare it retreat into ordinariness? Or pride? Or complacency? Or living unto itself? As if by our own right arm we had won ourselves this victory.

How does a nation progress and pray when suddenly it has become a symbol of hope to the continent of which it is part, as well as to a watching world?

One man of insight said, 'One has to go back a couple of centuries to find a historical happening of comparable wonder.' An Eastern leader has written, 'South Africa today holds the moral high ground. It has a unique opportunity. No other country in the world has South Africa's present standing and no other country can wield the same kind of influence.'

From pariah to paragon. From ultimate mess to ultimate model. From lost cause to guiding light. Overnight.

What is in South Africa's hands today, in the hands of both leaders and led, is a blossom of exquisite fragility. Handled with care, it will spread an aroma of goodness, hope and blessing across our planet. Man-handled or roughly held, it will fall to pieces to take its place in history's overflowing refuse bin of shattered dreams.

So what does a nation do when it has seen God work? How does it nurture this rare opportunity?

How then *should* we live?

TRANSITION

The question, I must admit, has thrust itself upon me since I saw the magic of Nelson Mandela's inauguration on 10 May 1994 as the first President of the new South Africa. What an astonishing transition from old order to new!

But then I hear the rumble of petty power-plays, of greed and acquisitiveness, of ongoing recrimination and the sounds of self-congratulation and once more I tremble. The heady wine of our own supposed success is going to our heads. And what does God think?

All this makes me fearful enough to have sought clues to answer this question and the way forward in this period of transition.

In my search for clues, a story from long ago has impressed itself upon me with hammer-like insistence.

A Biblical Clue

This story comes from the prophet Isaiah.

Isaiah grew up in the reign of the good King Uzziah, who ruled the southern kingdom of Judah in the eighth century BC. Judah had separated from the northern kingdom of Israel some two hundred years previously. Uzziah's reign had been a long one. Some fifty-two years. The nation had flourished, for the monarch was able and energetic. The rich had got richer. The poor, well, we're not sure.

But life without King Uzziah had become unthinkable. And then the unthinkable happened. Uzziah died.

Yet Isaiah records in stark simplicity, 'In the year that King Uzziah died, I saw the Lord.'[1] Judah's king had died. But Judah's God lived on. King Uzziah dies. But the King of Kings still sits upon His throne.

It was a moment then, as it is for South Africa now, to turn from all false and finite dependencies. For all are frail, all will vanish, all will fail. People and nations in every age have had to learn this.

In this year that King Apartheid died, we dare not depend on Nelson Mandela, nor upon a new Parliament, nor a new cabinet, nor the Government of National Unity, amazing as they may be. Our only dependency must be upon the Living God who has brought us thus far and who alone can lead us to His fulfilment of our national destiny.

Indeed our interim constitution declares in its preamble that, 'In humble submission to Almighty God, we the people of South Africa declare . . . ' As the new constitution is written, we need to remember what we have prayed for and what God has delivered us from. Let that declaration never be laid aside to accommodate the notion that as a nation we can ever live in any other way than in humble submission to Him.

It is because we may be tempted to do so that we, like Isaiah in post-Uzziah Judah, need to look beneath the surface.

Beneath the Surface

The prophet's reflections tell us that, underneath the surface success, there was 'a sinful nation, a people laden with iniquity', whose 'princes are rebels and companions of thieves' and where 'everyone loves a bribe and runs after gifts'.

People had become acquisitive and self-indulgent. Intellectual pride and self-sufficiency were also rampant, and therefore worthy of the prophet's rebuke: 'Woe to those who are wise in their own eyes and shrewd in their own sight.' People had even taken to 'calling evil good and good evil'. The occult was alive and well. Diviners and soothsayers were having a field day. Murder was commonplace. So was sexual looseness. And the poor were still being exploited.

Compared to the apartheid years, South Africa too looks pretty good on the surface. Yet in this time of transition, much that was in Judah in the eighth century BC is likewise with us in similar measure. And with similar perils to the survival of our privileged place as 'workshop of the world'. Many are embracing the view that to liberalise on race issues, as was so right and necessary, requires us also to abandon family values and liberalise on every issue relating to sexual behaviour, pornography, abortion on demand, Sunday observance, gambling, prostitution, and what is appropriate in the media and entertainment. Thus are we in danger of throwing out the baby of Judaeo-Christian values and ethics with the bathwater of apartheid.

Such moral laxity beneath the surface of our apparent political and social success in South Africa will imperil us as surely as it imperilled Judah immediately after Uzziah's death.

There also God's people had faced down giants in the land and won their God-given place in both history and geography. And they'd had God's word through prophets, poets, judges and kings. More than that, Planet Earth was waiting for the oracles of God through them, His instruments.

And then they began to lose it. God was politely saluted when it seemed convenient. But the path into the future was becoming a rut. Underneath, in the secret places where moral and spiritual choices are made, they were committing suicide.

It was the moment for both prophet and people, as with us in South Africa now, for –

A New Vision of God

How did Isaiah see God in the year that King Uzziah died?

First, he *saw Him 'sitting upon a throne, high and lifted up'*. This was not some tribal deity – or one in a pantheon of religious options. This was the God of all the universe. This was Yahweh. This was the Lord of Heaven and Earth, 'the Lord of Hosts' of whom it could be said that 'the whole earth is full of His glory'. This was the One who had said, 'I am the Lord your God, who brought you out of the land of Egypt, out of the house of bondage. You shall have no other gods before me.'[2]

Powerful stuff. And not easy to set aside. Then. Or now. Yes, Isaiah was seeing the King. Not King Uzziah. But the King of Kings. He could not get over it. 'My eyes have seen the King.' The One who is sovereign over the universe. And life. And history.

Second, Isaiah *saw God as worthy of worship*. The heavenly host are caught up in worship of this Lord. This One who had come before the prophet's sight was worthy to be praised, honoured, worshipped and adored. This One deserves all of a person's life and love. No allegiance of any sort can be higher than this – not to king or ruler, or president or party or people. They may have a portion of our devotion or allegiance, but nothing ultimate. That alone is reserved for the One Isaiah saw. The same One we've seen act so decisively in our own nation in these times.

Third, Isaiah *saw God as Holy and full of glory*. The heavenly host call to one another, 'Holy, Holy, Holy is the Lord of Hosts.'

This acclamation speaks of utter perfection in character and nature of the One we worship. Perfection of purity, justice, love and goodness. No flaw. No lies. No fallibility.

Isaiah had a vision of perfection, and of One standing in awful and awesome contrast to himself.

We in South Africa need to remember this. To remember who it is we have been interacting with. Who it is who has wrought in our land miracles that we have seen and touched. Isaiah was overwhelmed. As we should be. And it moved *him* from a fresh vision of God to –

A New Vision of Self and Nation

To see God in His kingly power, His worship-inspiring majesty and His perfect, awesome holiness is to be cast to the ground saying with the prophet, 'Woe is me! For I am lost: for I am a man of unclean lips and I live in the midst of a people of unclean lips.'

To see God as He is is to have a devastating encounter with ourselves in all our shabby sinfulness. For every part of us, even all our best and noblest endeavours, are infected with sin. Nothing we touch escapes its terrible, tainting ways.

We have seen what God is able to do in South Africa. If we see our God with new clarity, as we need to, we will see ourselves as unclean. And needing forgiveness, healing and divine help to move into the future with His enabling power lest our noblest political and social dreams are destroyed by the ungodliness in us who would pursue them.

To grasp this is not to take flights into morbidity or pessimism, but into reality, humility and the prevention of tragedy by the personal pursuit of God's grace and power.

And not just personal. It must be national too, for 'I dwell in the midst of a people of unclean lips'. In South Africa we have sought to shed our racism in some measure, but I see no mighty rush to biblical values, serious moral repentance, or the honouring of Jesus Christ and His Word and ways.

If it is indeed true that 'righteousness exalts a nation',[3] then righteousness should be pursued with all zeal and its opposite shunned with equal vigour.

And of course we need not just an understanding of national frailty and fallibility, but of national potential.

President Mandela, echoing Chief Albert Luthuli, put it this way: 'Here in South Africa, with all our diversities of colour and race, we will show the world a new pattern for democracy . . . I think there is a challenge for us in South Africa to set a new example for the world.'

Black Consciousness leader Steve Biko spoke of 'giving the world a more human face'.

Archbishop Desmond Tutu focuses on our challenge: 'We are to labour with God to help His children become ever more fully human which is a glorious destiny.'

What being fully human should be like we only see when, with prophets or apostles, we look into the face of God and of His Christ. And that is when we realise with Isaiah the need for and availability of –

A New Experience of Forgiveness

Amazingly, 'one of the seraphim' in Isaiah's vision flew to him with a burning, cleansing coal taken from the altar of God and touched Isaiah on his lips at the very point of his main and self-confessed sinfulness and pronounced, 'Your guilt is taken away, and your sin forgiven.'

Humans stand tallest when they know they are forgiven. Unhealed at that point they bear a mortal hurt. But to know that my dismal shabbiness, my dark thoughts or evil deeds and my utter inability to do anything but fall short not only of God's standards but my own, have all been seen and known and forgiven, even in the very moment of confession, ah, that is mystery indeed and marvellous beyond all the telling. It is too high for me to grasp. I cannot attain to it. It is nothing short of Amazing Grace. For it unblocks the barriers to our God and to one another and ushers us into light and love. Especially when we grasp that this God of ours is not just the God of Abraham, the hero of faith, and of Isaac, the perfect son, but of Jacob, the deceiver, supplanter and liar. Our God is the God of Jacob, too.

He is also the God and Father of our Lord Jesus Christ, the friend of sinners. How marvellous! Because how else could He be your friend or mine? How else could he lift life off its old hinges and give us a fresh start?

This is the heart of things. Forgiveness of sins. The Gospel which Jesus brought that leads us to life and immortality begins with forgiveness.

Yes, nothing in this lost world or in our broken nations bears so fully the impress of the Son of God as when His forgiveness reaches us and is passed from us to others. And pass it we must or we break the bridge over which we ourselves must pass. Everyone stands in need of forgiveness, and cannot receive it until they give it.

Perhaps in South Africa it is right that we must probe our past to see who has sinned against whom so that the truth may set us free. But let us do so knowing full well how delicate and precarious is that venture unless all sides know their own sinfulness and their own deep need for forgiveness. And what if when we ask who is speaking the truth we find all have lied at some time or other? Apartheid and all its works were full of evil. But resistance to it was not entirely devoid of evil either. The point is that unless our journey to the past takes us all to a merciful, forgiving God, we will not find healing and reconciliation but the fire-bombs of mutual recrimination which could blow our ship clean out of the water.

The search for truth must be embarked upon with the One who is the Truth so that He who knows the truth of the secrets of our hearts and actions may grant us, like Isaiah, a new experience of His forgiveness.

With that will come most wonderfully –

A New Experience of Hearing His Voice

No sooner had Isaiah been forgiven than he could report: 'I heard the voice of the Lord.'

Oh! Amazing happening to hear that voice and know what to do and how to move into the future. When sin is forgiven and out of the way, God's voice becomes audible.

I once called my dear, very deaf, elderly mother from the United States. Midway through the conversation she announced, 'Darling, it's absolutely marvellous to hear your voice, but I can't hear a word you're saying!'

Yes, it's marvellous to hear God's voice, but even more marvellous to hear what He is saying! For we need that guidance, lest we get wrong which way to go. Most especially do leaders need to hear so that we may have 'a leadership led by God'.

I recollect an experience in Oxford in 1980. I was walking the banks of the Isis River early one morning, praying about South Africa. So distinctly did I hear the Lord's voice within, I have never forgotten it: 'I have a way through for South Africa, but it will take a listening people.'

Some serious listening was perhaps done in the run-up to the South African elections in April 1994 and God had a way through for us. But we need an ongoing national lifestyle of listening to God as a people of prayer.

That will perhaps give birth in us to –

A New Sense of Vocation

The words Isaiah heard were, 'Whom shall I send and who will go for us?'

God is always looking for both individuals and nations to rise and offer themselves to Him to do His bidding.

John Henry Newman once wrote, 'God has created me

to do for Him some definite service: He has committed some work to me which He has not committed to another.'

It is so. And almost always it will be related to the good of others. Said Leo Tolstoy, 'The vocation of every man and woman is to serve other people.' Perhaps not an easy thing for all of us to hear in a nation so newly released from oppression.

South Africa, blessed in resources beyond many, dare not live just for itself. It must work and labour to bless Africa and the world. But especially Africa. If only for Africa's sake we dare not fail. Said a businessman in Kenya, 'As South Africa goes, so will go the rest of Africa.' Not only our national example, but our national helping hand is needed if Africa is to come through.

Do we want to do it? We can, for we have as never before –

A New Opportunity to Offer Ourselves for Service

The first words from Isaiah's freshly forgiven and newly touched lips were monumental and they have rung across the arches of the years like a thunderclap. 'Here am I! Send me!'

Monosyllabic. But titanic. Here is poor, inadequate, weak, sinful humanity on the line for God. Not very able. But available. And here is divine condescension stooping majestically in love to say, 'Go'.

Isaiah's mission was tough. For it was to rebuke a rebellious people. Ours might be less arduous. Or more. Who knows?

But the chance is there individually and nationally to do something beautiful for God and for His Christ. Here in the Beloved Country. Also out there in our convulsive but incredible continent. And in the wider world.

South Africa should do it. So that our witness is not just for a fleeting, magic moment of extraordinary time, but for ever.

Notes

Chapter 1
1 *The Independent* (London), 'The sun shall never set on so glorious a human achievement', text of Nelson Mandela's inaugural speech, 11 May 1994.

Chapter 2
1 Allister Sparks, *The Star*, Johannesburg, 6 October 1993.

Chapter 3
1 Call which came to the Apostle Paul from Macedonia to 'Come over and help us' (Acts 16:9).
2 *Natal Witness*, 'Border bloodbath', 8 September 1992.
3 *Natal Witness*, 'Brigadier Gqozo kicked out', 9 September 1992.
4 Benny Alexander has now changed his name to Khoisan X.

Chapter 4
1 In 1957, 156 people including Nelson Mandela and South African Communist Party Leader, Braam Fisher, were put on trial for high treason. Most received lengthy sentences, some of them for life as was the case with Nelson Mandela.
2 Quoted in *The Hodder Book of Christian Quotations*, Hodder and Stoughton, London, 1982, p. 89.
3 *The Ossewa Brandwag* (or Ox-Wagon Sentinel) was an Afrikaner organisation founded in Bloemfontein in 1938. Its original purpose was to preserve the moral values and idealism of the Great Trek and safeguard the traditions of the Afrikaners. It was also to serve as a rallying point for all true-blue Afrikaners who wanted to share in these goals. Initially it professed indifference to politics. But it developed almost into a shadow defence force and a vehicle for radical Afrikaner nationalism.

Chapter 6
1 Editorial by van Zyl Slabbert, *Democracy in Action*, Aug/Sept 1990.

2 *Democracy in Action* (Journal of the Institute for Democracy in South Africa), interview with Alex Boraine by Sue Valentine, 'From Dakar to Democracy', Vol. 8, No. 4, 15 July 1994, pp. 10–11.

3 *ibid*.

4 *Financial Mail*, 'The honest brokers', 29 April 1994, p. 20.

5 *The Road to Rustenburg: The Church looking forward to a new South Africa*, Dr Louw Alberts and Rev. Dr Frank Chikane, editors, Cape Town, Struik Christian Books Ltd, 1991, p. 14.

6 *ibid*., p. 14.

7 *ibid*., p. 14.

8 *ibid*., p. 14.

9 *ibid*., p. 15.

10 *ibid*., p. 92.

11 *ibid*., p. 16.

12 *ibid*., Rustenburg Declaration, Clause 4.3, pp. 283–4.

13 The full text of the historic National Peace Accord is available from their offices, 344 Vine Avenue, Ferndale 2194.

Chapter 7
1 *Tragedy to Triumph*, Bishop Frank Retief, Nelson Ward Ltd, Milton Keynes, Struik Books Ltd, Cape Town, 1994, p.25.

Chapter 8
1 'Blundering towards calamity', John Kane-Berman, *Natal Witness*, 18 March 1993.

2 *Natal Witness*, 2 January 1993.

3 *Natal Witness*, 9 January 1993.

4 *Natal Witness*, 25 January 1993.

5 *Race Relations Survey*, Carole Cooper et al, Research Staff, South African Institute of Race Relations, SAIRR, Johannesburg, 1994, pp. 297–8

6 *Natal Witness*, 3 March 1993.

7 *ibid*.

8 *Natal Witness*, 9 March 1993.

9 *Natal Witness*, 22 March 1993.

10 'Seeing through the gloom', Allister Sparks, *Natal Witness*, 25 March 1993.

11 *ibid*.

12 *ibid*.

13 *Natal Witness*, 15 April 1993.

14 *Natal Witness*, 21 April 1993.

15 *Natal Witness*, 8 May 1993.

16 *Natal Witness*, 10 May 1993.

17 *Natal Witness*, 13 May 1993.

18 'Zulu Ethnicity Unheeded' by Heribert Adam, *Natal Witness*, Monday, 11 April 1994.

19 *Natal Witness*, 15 June 1993.
20 *Natal Witness*, 5 July 1993.
21 *Natal Witness*, 6 July 1993.
22 *Natal Witness*, 27 October 1993.
23 *Natal Witness*, 4 November 1993.
24 *Natal Witness*, 9 November 1993.
25 *Natal Witness*, 10 November 1993.
26 *Natal Witness*, 7 December 1993.
27 *Natal Witness*, 11 December 1993.
28 *Natal Witness*, 14 December 1993.
29 *Natal Witness*, 16 December 1993.
30 *Natal Witness*, 17 December 1993.
31 *Natal Witness*, 18 December 1993.
32 *Natal Witness*, 21 December 1993.
33 *Natal Witness*, 22 December 1993.
34 *Natal Witness*, 23 December 1993.
35 *Natal Witness*, 28 December 1993.

Chapter 9

1 Those participating in leadership of the day were:
Chairman: Archbishop Wilfrid Napier, Archbishop of Durban.
Keynote Speakers
Rev. Dr Khoza Mgojo, Ex-President of Methodist Church of Southern Africa, President of South African Council of Churches.
Mr Michael Cassidy, Founder and International Team Leader, African Enterprise.
Bishop Stanley Mogoba, Presiding Bishop of Methodist Church of Southern Africa.
Mr Anthony Ardington, Chairman, Russell, Marriott and Boyd Trust.
Dr Nkosazana Zuma, Medical Doctor and Head of ANC Southern Natal Health Department.
Dr Lynn Hurry, Consultant, Institute of Natural Resources, University of Natal.
Dr Mike Jarvis, Director, Education Management, Natal Education Department.
Panel Members
Rev. Nic Addison, Chairman of Policy Committee, African Christian Democratic Party.
The Hon Mr George Bartlett, Natal Leader, National Party.
Mr Roger Burrows, Natal Leader, Democratic Party.
Dr Ziba Jiyane, Political Director, Inkatha Freedom Party.
Mr Armichand Rajbansi, Leader, Minority Front.
Dr Selva Saman, Secretary for Health, Pan Africanist Congress.
Mr Jacob Zuma, Deputy Secretary-General, African National Congress.

2 *Sarie*, 'Die Engel in ons huis', Marina Möller, 25 May 1994, pp. 34–5 (translated by Heidi Jones).
3 *Sunday Times*, 'Angelic Vision sparks off national prayer for peace', Monica Oosterbroek, 10 April 1994.

Chapter 11
1 *Boston Sunday Globe*, 1 May 1994.
2 *Daily News*, 20 April 1994.
3 *Sunday Tribune*, 24 April 1994.
4 *Natal Witness*, 20 April 1994.

Chapter 12
1 Isaiah 6:1.
2 Exodus 20:2–3.
3 Proverbs 14:34.

Index